GET RISKY OR
GET LOST

Get Risky or Get Lost

The Psychology, Science and Art of Precision Risk-Taking

Chizubel E. Beluchi

Published by Game Changer Publishing

Paperback ISBN: 978-1-964811-42-0
Hardcover ISBN: 978-1-964811-43-7
Digital ISBN: 978-1-964811-44-4

www.GameChangerPublishing.com

DEDICATION

This book is lovingly dedicated to my father, Patrick A.O. Egwudo, who took the risk in the midst of heavy fighting during the Nigerian-Biafran civil war in 1967 to reach the United Kingdom through extreme circumstances, creating an opportunity for us. It was my mission to finish this book before your time on earth is complete. This book is your reward.

Get Risky or Get Lost

The Psychology, Science and Art
of Precision Risk-Taking

Chizubel E. Beluchi

www.GameChangerPublishing.com

Author's Note

'You are two things when you are born: a human being
and a risk-taker. That is a gift!'

The world has become an increasingly complex place for everyone, regardless of status. The so-called ordinary person struggles to get through each day, and in some cases, by any means necessary to make a living, while the rich continue to amass obscene amounts of wealth as their way of mitigating the downturn of humanity we are experiencing despite technological and scientific 'advancement.' If we all are human beings and risk-takers, why do we have such disparities in potential?

My reason for writing *Get Risky or Get Lost* is two-fold. *First,* to provide the world with a guide to achieving their purpose. *Second*, to unveil the truth about risk, with crystal clear explanations that lift the lid on known and unknown facts that are hidden. The lessons herein are important for beginning to know how we can overcome common obstacles that become part of 'human nature' and are overlooked as being normal but, in reality, individually and collectively amalgamate into avoidable disasters.

–Chizubel E. Beluchi, July 2024

Foreword

By Sebastian Jung

When I first met Chizubel. E. Beluchi at a summer course at the CG Jung Institute in Zurich, Switzerland, we instantly connected. Curious about his background, I asked what brought him to the institute. He explained that he is a risk strategist delving deeper into psychology to better understand the conscious and unconscious drivers of risk and its importance for individual and organisational transformation.

One of my earliest and most unusual memories of Chizubel E. Beluchi involves a dream work session with the renowned Jungian analyst Dr. Art Funkhouser. We were sitting in the basement of the institute, surrounded by thick, old stone walls. When Dr. Funkhouser asked who wanted to share their dream with the group, Chizubel's hand shot up immediately. He said he had a dream he needed to share before leaving the room. As Chizubel began to recount his dream, we were all captivated by his vivid, detailed storytelling. The dream transported us to his childhood in Africa, filled with vibrant colours, rituals and mystique. The imagery was so powerful that it has stayed with me ever since.

After the seminar, I shared with him my work as an organisational consultant and leadership coach at Como Consult and leading the R&D work at the Presencing Institute, co-founded by Dr. Otto Scharmer, MIT Sloan and global thought leader who had written Theory U – Leading from the Emerging Future. My focus lies on transformation processes and systems evolution in organisations for which I develop enabling methodologies. This involves pushing the boundaries of the present and sensing future possibilities that are not yet fully realised in our current systems. Chizubel then asked me if I would become his sparring partner in developing a cutting-edge model that integrates risk with the pursuit of purpose aimed at facilitating organisational transformation. I was thrilled at the prospect.

The Many Facets of Risk

Before our collaboration began, I was intrigued by the origins of the word risk and its implications in modern management literature and practice. Risk impacts decisions at every level, from personal choices to global economies.

The Oxford dictionary reveals that risk is defined as the possibility of something bad happening in the future; a situation that could be dangerous or have a negative outcome. In Western contexts, risk often signifies something to be minimised for stability, emphasising the potential for loss or harm. Similarly, risk management is described as the process of identifying financial risks and planning strategies to mitigate them. This definition underscores the prevailing view that managing risk involves systematically reducing future threats through careful planning.

However, as Chizubel once highlighted to me, this perspective represents only one facet of risk. Risk entails more than mere avoidance of problems; it encompasses embracing opportunities and navigating uncertainties for growth and innovation.

Integrating Western And Eastern Origins of Risk

My interest was sparked, prompting me to delve into the origins of the word risk and its true meanings. The etymology of risk is captivating, spanning languages and centuries. It traces back through Latin and Italian roots, where risk is believed to originate from the early Italian word risicare, meaning to dare. This Italian term derives from the Latin *'risicum'*, which denotes hazard or peril, especially in maritime navigation. Some scholars suggest that *'risicum'* in Latin may have its roots in the Greek word *'rhiza'*, meaning root, stone, or cut off from the firm shore, evoking the image of navigating treacherous waters near rocky coasts. Thus, from its etymological journey, risk teaches us about the courage to navigate dangerous paths, forging through uncertain terrain.

This metaphor of navigating perilous waters holds true in today's fast-paced world. Understanding and managing risk is more crucial than ever before. The concept of VUCA—Volatility, Uncertainty, Complexity, and Ambiguity—captures the essence of the leadership challenges we face today in managing risk. This demands flexible strategies, resilience, agility, ongoing learning, and adaptive leadership.

In Eastern traditions, particularly in Chinese, the word for risk, 危机 (wēijī), encapsulates both danger (危) and opportunity (机). This reflects a cultural perspective that sees risk as inherently linked to both potential harm and potential gain. Rooted in traditional Chinese philosophy, which values the balance of opposites like Yin and Yang, it emphasises not just avoiding danger but also identifying and leveraging opportunities within risky situations.

While Western approaches often seek to minimise or control uncertainty, Francois Jullien's interpretation of Chinese thought suggests that uncertainty is not necessarily seen as purely negative. Instead, it can be viewed as an opportunity for creativity, innovation, and unexpected outcomes. This perspective encourages a more open-minded approach to risk, where uncertainty becomes a space for exploration and growth rather than solely a threat to be managed.

Risk 2.0: Risk Is A Person Or An Entity With A Purpose

Chizubel E. Beluchi's second book, *GET RISKY OR GET LOST: The Psychology, Science and Art of Precision Risk-Taking*, stands out in the field of 'risk' literature for its innovative approach. It advocates for a proactive and creative handling of risk, acknowledging the close connection between threats and opportunities.

In his comprehensive approach to risk, Chizubel breaks it down into two major components: Risk Exploitation (Opportunities & Rewards) and Risk Management (Threats & Issues). This dual framework emphasises both the proactive identification and pursuit of opportunities inherent in risk and the traditional focus on mitigating potential threats. By integrating these perspectives, he provides a holistic view that fosters innovation while maintaining vigilance against adverse outcomes.

What sets this author's approach apart is his emphasis on personal responsibility in both risk exploitation and risk management, encapsulated in his core definition: '"Risk" is a person or entity with a purpose'. This perspective underscores that risk is inherent in all human endeavours that seek to fulfil a goal or purpose. In today's ever-changing world, risk is no longer just a hazard to be mitigated or an obstacle to be avoided. The author has evolved it into a dynamic concept—Risk 2.0—where risk is perceived as an individual or entity represented as organisations, companies or businesses with a defined purpose.

Purpose defines our reason for existence, whether for individuals or entities like organisations and businesses, regardless of their size. It addresses fundamental questions: *Why am I here? What am I living for? What value do I offer? How do I contribute to improving lives on this planet?* Clarifying these answers is pivotal in defining your purpose, which Mr Beluchi shows step by step in his first book, *For the Love of Purpose*.

Discover What Kind Of Risk-Taker You Are

How we deal with risk differs widely between each of us. Successful people are often willing to take high risks to achieve extraordinary things. What kind of risk-taker are you? With the concept of multiple personalities of risk, Chizubel explores how individuals exhibit varying responses to risk across different situations. Whether one is an active risk taker, a passive observer within their comfort zone, an accidental opportunist, a hybrid of active and passive strategies, a high-stakes material risk taker, or a dynamic integrator of all these approaches, understanding one's dominant risk personality is crucial for navigating opportunities effectively and achieving defined purposes. Knowing your strengths and weaknesses aids personal development and team dynamics. Understanding the connection between your own comfort zones, risk, uncertainty, and growth is vital for personal and organisational development. Comfort zones are our familiar, safe routines, while growth occurs when we step into uncertain situations beyond these boundaries, into a kind of liminal space of unfamiliar territory. This involves taking risks, as new opportunities come with uncertainty.

Bridging The Philosophy And Psychology Of Risk

In his wide exploration of the world of risk, Chizubel also delves into the intersection of philosophy and psychology as vital tools for understanding and navigating risk. Risk philosophy involves studying the environmental, economic, and social dynamics that shape human existence, while risk psychology focuses on comprehending human behaviour and using this insight to pursue purpose effectively. By recognising and overcoming systemic and psychological barriers, individuals can harness their conscious and unconscious minds to achieve transformative outcomes. This book offers practical insights and strategies to align personal and organisational goals with purpose, facilitating a path towards meaningful success.

The Future Of Risk: A New Operating System Is Needed

As our world undergoes rapid and unprecedented changes, our approach to risk must evolve accordingly. Traditional risk management systems primarily focus on mitigating negative outcomes. This focus has become increasingly outdated in a fast-paced, interconnected world. When you consider the Eastern practice of risk, which dates back hundreds of centuries, far older than the Western approach, you get to see the reason why Chizubel is resolved in pursuing his mission to bring a more accurate version of risk to the world that combines both opportunity and crisis management leading to the achievement of a defined purpose. These frameworks, once effective, now act as barriers, stifling innovation and agility by prioritising risk avoidance over opportunity exploration.

The Western way of risk, which is commercially available, fails to meet the unique needs of individuals and organisations today. In contrast, the emerging approach of Risk 2.0, which Chizubel is a proponent of, emphasises recognising and seizing opportunities inherent in risk. This approach is coupled with personal self-knowledge and leadership skills to better understand yourself as a risk-taker and foster innovation. It requires new, tailored operating systems with structures, processes, and practices that equip organisations, teams, and individuals, helping them become aware of the unique specificities and their behaviours around risk and create strategies that help them fulfil their purpose.

As you read Mr Chizubel Beluchi's new book, you will be compelled to upgrade your understanding of risk because your discovery is essential for the transformation needed for the achievement of purpose on a personal level and global level.

-Sebastian Jung, Santiago de Chile

---

*Sebastian Jung is an organisational consultant and leadership coach at Como Consult and leads the R&D work at the Presencing Institute. The institute was co-founded by Dr. Otto Scharmer, MIT Sloan and global thought leader who wrote Theory U—Leading from the Emerging Future.

Table of Contents

CHAPTER ONE

Get Risky or Get Lost

On 16 April 2016, my reputation was on the line. I had taken on a project to deliver a two-day risk training in Kuala Lumpur, Malaysia, to senior executives from across East Asia. I had less than a month between the time I agreed to the project and the time I had to deliver the training. I said yes, not thinking about the messy divorce I was going through, my workload, and an important client (a multinational investment bank I was consulting with) at the time. All expenses were paid with fees. I was excited, but not because of the money: It was my first international gig as a risk consultant and an excellent distraction from all the legal wranglings of the divorce.

Fast forward to the day I had to fly out. I got to the airport that Saturday morning for my flight at 9 a.m. I walked up to the check-in counter and realised I had forgotten my passport at home. Add this to the issue that I had no slides developed or material to deliver my training, and I thought, *What a big flop!* I had just lost the one full day I had to prepare my material before the training on Monday. I thought *I might as well just call them up and give some flimsy excuse that I can no longer deliver the training.* I was faced with the choice of whether to get risky or get lost. I chose to get risky, and the opportunities started to present themselves. Getting lost was not an option for me, with a whole team of support staff and delegates waiting for me and a chauffeur calling to ask when I would be arriving. It could have been a disaster, but I was not going to allow this challenge to ruin my reputation and my future as a leader in the field of risk. It was my defining moment psychologically and, ultimately, for my greater purpose.

To wrap this story up, there was an Emirates flight out at 2 p.m. that afternoon. I paid for it, got a rental car, drove home to pick up my passport, and came back to the airport for my flight later that day. One thing I did not do was worry; my mind was busy with problem-solving and creating the layout of my training material. As I got on the flight to Kuala Lumpur, I was so mentally tired that I decided to eat a meal, drink some wine, and sleep because I knew this was going to be the only rest I would have. Somewhere mid-flight, I worked on my slides a little.

I was picked up by the chauffeur late Sunday afternoon, as I had rearranged my pickup time. I was taken to my lush hotel, had a shower, had dinner, and got to work. I pounded out my material all night to get the Day One presentation ready for my grand delivery. Finishing at around 5 a.m., I had only two hours of sleep, and I got ready. Thankfully, the jet lag had not set in yet. I delivered Day One, and it was a hit, with new relationships formed that I still maintain to this day.

I repeated the process on day two. And then it hit me—I was fighting jet lag. Right in the middle of the morning session, someone asked me a question while I was microsleeping with my eyes open. I did not comprehend what was being asked of me. I was not going to fall on my face now after all it took to get here. I snapped out of it with a short burst of energy and got to work. In the end, I made it through, successfully delivering one of my best trainings to date.

Why am I telling you this story? You see, anyone, and I mean anyone, has the ability to take risks and achieve their purpose no matter what circumstances you find yourself in. Strength and opportunities come when you have made a commitment to something or someone. What you need to know is that your appetite for risk-taking will only be commensurate with the purpose you are seeking to achieve. The question you must ask yourself now is, *What is my purpose? Is it significant enough and appropriate to what I am capable of?*

To take risks, you must first understand a few fundamental principles. Unfortunately, these are not taught by the education system or most other programmes—academic or professional.

Whether you are the CEO of a major corporation, the leader of a government world power, or an immigrant crossing the sea from Africa to get to Europe, we are all born risk-takers and have the ability to succeed in life. The sad reality is that many have allowed environmental conditions to lobotomise them into playing it safe and falling into the cursed state called the 'comfort zone', tippy-toeing through life until death without really contributing what they can to humanity.

This is the state that most of the world's population and organisations are in—and are forever trying to get out of.

You might be wondering why I have dedicated my time to writing a book on risk. To answer your question, it would be a big sin if I did not share this with the world after coming to know what I am about to share with you in this book. As I take you through this book, I will teach you the fundamentals of life, that is, the fundamentals of risk and risk-taking that you need to know, which will change your life. Let us get right into it.

A Life of Risk

My whole life has been a risk. Events that happened in my life when I was a child and how I handled them were all part of the process of responding to the risks I was unknowingly living and taking. My consciousness about risk was awakened as I researched the profession of risk, and it was further intensified when I started to explore more deeply into psychology to understand the conscious and unconscious drivers of and for risk. I was unravelling truths, lies, and realities, aligning two disciplines (risk and psychology) that are glaringly related but disconnected in practice and likely responsible for most of the way the world is today—particularly the world of business and commerce. In 2017, when I first started writing this book, I had to set it aside to work on another book project to allow my thoughts to marinate and become more seasoned.

After dedicating two decades so far to studying, learning, understanding, and practising risk, I concluded that risk has two main constants: people and the actions you take. Without people, risk would not exist. Without actions, you cannot achieve a purpose.

I have been exposed to the truth and lies of risk, knowing what a vast majority of people do not know, and I must say, it is empowering. Take, for example, a virtual meeting I had in late 2023 with the Chief Operating Officer of a well-known wealth management company and her direct reports. She mentioned the picture on the wall behind me in my office, which bears the slogan 'THE RISK IS YOU'. I strategically positioned this thought-provoking picture there so that whenever I have virtual meetings, it inspires a conversation. In this case, it did, and what resulted from this experience was a confirmation that what most people know about risk is wrong. Let us start with the biggest lie about risk ever told and the impact this has had on the world.

The Big Lies About Risk

- 'Risk is a potential negative waiting to happen.' Lie.
- 'Risk is uncertainty.' Lie.
- 'Risk is the probability of a good or bad outcome.' Lie.
- 'Risk is dangerous.' Lie.
- 'Risk is the possibility of an investor experiencing loss due to factors that affect the overall performance of the financial market (Investopedia).' Lie.
- 'Risk can be defined as the combination of the probability of an event and its consequences (The Institute of Risk Management).' Lie.

- 'An uncertain event or condition that, if it occurs, has a positive or negative effect on a project's objective (Project Management Institute PMBOK Guide).' Half-truth that is a lie.
- '[Risk is] the possibility that the occurrence of an event will adversely affect the achievement of the organisation's objectives (Stanford University).' Lie.
- 'Risk is the probability of an outcome having a negative effect on people, systems, or assets (United Nations Office for Disaster Risk Reduction).' Lie.
- 'Risk is a known unknown.' What a big fat poop of a lie. Whoever came up with that should be sent into exile on another planet.

These are some of the lies being perpetrated about risk that have misled the world into how risk is perceived or understood and should not be taken lightly. You have to ask yourself, *Why are we being told all these lies, misinformation, and half-truths about risk?*

The shocking and sad reality is that these misleading ideas have shaped the world extensively and have led to many corporations failing badly, people being kept in poverty, and at levels of mediocrity that are believed to be a normal way of life, with no way out. The problem with these definitions of risk is that they transfer ownership of risk to an external party, to someone else or something else. So what really is 'risk'?

The Truth About Risk

Risk is a person or an entity with a purpose. You see, for many years in my work as a risk consultant, I believed the lies and misinformation about risk. But it never really made sense. Especially when I saw how top company executives paid lip service to risk and never took it seriously despite spending money to bring in who they perceived to be the best consultants and strategists to implement risk frameworks and processes that did not align with the purpose they wanted to achieve. It was in 2017 that it dawned on me, as I explored psychology, that risk is us—you and me. Without people, there is no risk. People create entities (organisations, companies, institutions, and businesses), and by default, these entities become the risk. We all have a purpose as individuals, whether we know it or not. Every entity has a purpose, whether it is clearly defined or not. An entity can be made up of one person or hundreds of people who are part of that one entity.

Let us examine risk more closely in light of this new definition. While we do so, I want you to ask yourself, does this definition make sense to you? That definition again is: **Risk is a person or an entity with a purpose.** I am going to repeat this definition at several points throughout this book to demonstrate its accuracy with several examples.

To support your understanding, I want you to put yourself in this definition. These are not just words because, in reality, you, the person or entity in pursuit of a purpose, are required to take action to achieve it. How you go about it determines the outcome you get in relation to your purpose, whether it be success or failure. Simply put, risk equals you.

You might be wondering, *How then, do the different types of risk fit into this new understanding of risk?* Things like people risk, investment risk, environmental risk, money risk, business risk, and so on, which all have been associated with the potential for loss. This next section will clarify that for you.

The 80/20 Rule of Risk

The 80/20 Rule of Risk is an adaptation of Pareto's principle, also known as the 80/20 rule, which states that for many events, roughly 80% of effects come from 20% of the causes.

The 80/20 Rule of Risk is different. The rule states that 'the sum of a person's or entity's risk is the combination of Risk Exploitation and Risk Management needed to successfully achieve a defined purpose.' If all your risk activities equal 100%, 80% of your risk activities should be focused on risk exploitation, and the remaining 20% should be focused on risk management.

What is the difference between risk exploitation and risk management? Risk exploitation is your upside of risk, which is the combination of all your opportunities and the rewards derived, while risk management is the combination of all the threats you are exposed to and the problems you have. The next section will discuss the four variants of risk.

What you need to understand is that risk exploitation consists of quantifiable activities and measurable results that deliver your purpose. Without them, there will be no growth, and you will fade out of existence. Risk management consists of activities and events you perform that ringfence you or your purpose, protecting you from both internal and external influences that could negatively affect you, thereby creating losses.

The Four Variants of Risk

The way to understand risk further is to think of yourself, the human being. You are one human being. Inside you, you have the cells that constitute you as a person, from stem cells to bone cells, blood cells, sperm cells, female egg cells, and so on. The cells in your body are different, but they form you, the one human being.

It is the same with risk. You could say that there are four main cells or variants of risk: *opportunity cells, reward cells, threat cells,* and *issue cells,* all forming one body—risk. Let me explain these variants and their functions to help you better grasp the full truth about risk.

Opportunity

Opportunities are the potential rewards or benefits identified but not yet received. This is the biggest and most important variant of risk and could be said to be the life force or life source to your purpose. Without you being given an opportunity at life through birth, you would not exist to experience the various aspects of life. **Risk is a person or an entity with a purpose.** You became a risk when you were conceived, giving you an opportunity in life to fulfil a purpose. Your company, organisation, or business became a risk when it was formed because it identified opportunities to fulfil a purpose, regardless of whether it is a good one or a bad one. You start something—a business, a company, an organisation, or embark on an expedition—because of the opportunity to derive a benefit from it.

I like to use the example of discovering gold, as I think most people can relate to this. Imagine having a little piece of land, whether it is in your garden or your farm. You have one of those sensors that scan for metals, and it indicates that you have hit gold. You are excited, and you think of the potential. The potential of how much money you can make, for example, and so on. But that is what they are—just potential. That is because you have to take action to convert the opportunity (the gold you have found) before it can serve you. For opportunities to serve you best, it is vital that you know their structure. There are opportunities you must seize now, opportunities you have to monitor and wait for, opportunities you must create for yourself, and opportunities that are given to you, as well as opportunities from misfortune. Opportunities from misfortune are often overlooked, but to successfully take risks, one must see opportunity in everything. I talk more about this in chapter three.

Response for Opportunities: Convert them to rewards.

Reward

Rewards are real-time benefits that you can measure. The action you take to convert an opportunity to a measurable benefit gives you the reward you desire. In the example of discovering gold as an opportunity, you took action, exploited the opportunity by digging the ground to get the gold, and converted the gold by selling it at a value you feel it is worth, depending on its size and quantity. The money you get when you sell the gold is your reward for the hard work and intelligence that went into discovering and extracting the gold from the ground. The benefits you get in money can now be used to do whatever you please. You, the risk, are on the path to achieving your purpose due to the successful conversion and value of the benefits you are receiving.

Response for Rewards: Measure the value generated. Reinvest a value. Enjoy the rewards.

Threat

Threats are potential problems, whether identified or not, which have the probability of causing you problems if they were to transpire. Problems such as loss of time, loss of money, imprisonment, ruined reputation, and death are just a few examples. To prevent these threats from happening or to minimise the damage they could cause, you need to put some control measures in place.

Let us use the example of driving a car. There is always the threat of an accident happening when you drive—an identified or known threat. To prevent or minimise the likelihood of an accident, you make sure your tyres are in good condition, your brakes work, your windshield wipers function, your steering wheel operates correctly, and, most importantly, you drive safely. These control measures should reduce the likelihood of the threat of an accident becoming real, saving you from injury, time lost, money loss, or even your life. These are the dynamics of threats in any given situation or establishment.

I mentioned earlier various types of risk, such as people risk, investment risk, environmental risk, money risk, business risk, operational risk, and many others. What people infer is the potential for some sort of damage happening in these areas of risk. The use of the word 'risk' is a blanket approach taken by many to mean the potential of something unpleasant or bad happening, which is not correct, as I have shown you through the definition of risk that it 'is a person or an entity with a purpose'. Therefore, the action you take on a threat should protect your purpose from the possibility of a negative risk impact. If we take investment risk, for example, when you invest in a stock, there is the likelihood of a loss or a gain. The steps you take to prevent a loss means that the chances of achieving your investment purpose is higher.

Response for Threats: Mitigate them with controls.

Issue

Issues are real-time problems affecting you now and causing you trouble. You are losing money, your marriage is falling apart, someone just ran into your car from behind, or your dog just died. These are ninety-nine problems you just do not want to have, but they are killing you right now with sleepless nights and stress, making you want to pull your hair out. Okay, I was exaggerating a little, but you get the point, I am sure. One thing you need to know about issues is that they are designed to create ruin, destroy, and obliterate you, the person or the entity when they happen.

What you need to understand is that the severity of an issue or problem can be determined based on the controls you had in place for the threat that created the problem. Weak or no control measures means that the problem could have a more detrimental effect on you. In addition, the effectiveness of the resolution activities or contingency plans for an issue can determine how quickly they are resolved. Performing scenario analysis can help you anticipate problems so that you can be ready if or when they happen. See Chapter Eight for more on Scenario Analysis and how to use it.

Response for Issues: Resolve them.

Figure 1. The Risk Diagram

Why You Need to Get Risky

Every human being is born a risk-taker. From the baby born somewhere in the world just this minute to the person who lives in a poorly developed nation to the CEO of the richest corporation on earth—we are all risk-takers. Your level of risk-taking is determined by the purpose that you define and immerse yourself in through alignment. The value of this purpose is determined by your desire and risk-taking in relation to the purpose. Whether you are an organisation, a business, or an individual, if your purpose is not compelling enough or you do not have a clearly defined purpose, you will be in a constant state of reaction and eventually become irrelevant to the world around you, dying off either metaphorically or literally. Having a clearly defined purpose is fundamental to risk-taking. To put it another way: your purpose is fundamental to your existence and the impact you have on the world's stage at any level, small or great.

When I see beggars on the street, I often wonder, *Who would these people be if they had a compelling purpose and were driven by their risk-taking appetite to pursue that purpose? Could these individuals have been scientists, doctors, entrepreneurs, chief executives, or musicians?* We walk past them every day. Next time you walk past a beggar, think about them in this capacity and ask yourself, *How different am I from them? Am I a symbolic beggar who just takes from the resources the world offers and gives back nothing of what I should? What is my purpose, and what am I doing to achieve it?* If you do not have a clearly defined purpose, you are not taking risks purposefully and everything you do could be likened to running around aimlessly, being no different from these beggars.

What It Means to Get Risky

The term 'risky' has, for a very long time, been used in a negative context to denote the possibility of an unfavourable event happening due to a person's action. Let us get one thing very clear: To be in a risky state does not mean you are in a dangerous situation or that you are embarking on something that will end in disaster. 'Getting risky' or taking risks means that you are action-bound towards a purpose. Remember our definition of risk above—that you are the risk aligned to a purpose. It is in its natural order: risk and then purpose, or risk is equal to purpose. You are going to hear this repeated a few times in this book.

To get risky is your readiness to find the opportunities associated with your purpose and then convert those opportunities to the rewards or benefits that actualise your purpose. While doing this, you actively anticipate potential problems that can prevent your purpose from being fulfilled and put in place measures to protect your purpose and the investments you are putting into it so that you have a high success ratio. In doing so, you are dynamically operating all the cylinders of risk in relation to your purpose, taking the respective actions needed. These actions need to be consistent regardless of the challenges you are presented with.

Know Your Risk Territory

Your risk territory is the environment in which you operate to achieve your purpose. Just like a child at a playground who knows virtually every facility and eagerly explores them to get the utmost fun out of the playground, you need to know your risk territories—from your place of operation to the places where your purpose will materialise. A thought that starts in the mind can have a far-reaching impact beyond the point of origin of the individual having that thought. This is where the power of visualisation has to be practised until the purpose is achieved.

For an individual, this is easy because you only have yourself to think about in relation to where you live and work. For a much larger entity such as an organisation, it is far more complex because it may impact a much wider audience and geography beyond its place of origin. Aligning them requires much more work to ensure they understand the risk territory beyond the location of the organisation's premises.

As the CEO, you need to have the mindset of a military general. Before going on a mission to accomplish a purpose, they educate the battalion (employees) on the mission at hand; otherwise, they would be sending them to their graves. They must understand the purpose: protect the country, conquer land, bring back the 'booty' such as gold and so on. Then, through surveillance and other military strategies, the general would have gathered military intelligence that needs to be inculcated in the minds of the soldiers, such as vital reconnaissance information about the enemy's base or the place that needs to be conquered. In a similar way, knowing the immediate scope of your risk territory is vital, not just for the achievement of your purpose but also for the maintenance of it.

Your risk territory can be the city you live in, where your company is based, where your target audience are, and even wider. These environments change with time, so part of knowing your risk territory involves adapting to the changing times in relation to your purpose. We will explore this in Chapter Four, detailing the vital aspects of what your risk territory must have for you to achieve your purpose.

Multiple Personalities of Risk

Every person is two things when they are born: a *human being and a risk-taker.* You survived the environment of the womb you were carried in, and the external factors you had no control over, that is, the actions of your mother, whether good or bad, and then you were born into the world. Congratulations to you. Often, congratulations go to the mother, but congratulations to you, too.

You see, multiple personalities are not disorders, as we are made to believe. As humans, we are designed with multiple abilities and psychological response mechanisms that, when brought together, can project what seems like a different personality in a given situation. Take, for example, a stranger who gives you a box of chocolates with a smile. How do you respond compared to when a family member or friend gives you a box of chocolates with a smile? Would it be the same? Your response is determined by several pieces of information you processed to make your decision about the stranger and the box of chocolates. Who are you at that point when the stranger approaches and gives you a box of chocolates versus when a family member does? Multiple personalities of you, or just you being who you need to be in each situation to achieve a given purpose? Sometimes, we are active in risk-taking and other times, we are not. Understanding the multiple personalities of risk will enable you to know your dominant personality and how to activate the power source you need to achieve your purpose in any situation and environment you are in. Let us examine each risk personality type and, while doing so, learn what each one is, which one represents your dominant personality, and how and when to use each one or combine them.

The Active Risk-Taker

The active risk-taker is the person who consciously takes risks. People with this personality type know that to achieve their purpose, they have to invest their time, their bodies, their minds, their money, and/or their family. Pretty much whatever it takes to achieve the purpose, they will put in that effort to do it. That is the mindset of an active risk-taker. Do not misunderstand this. Stock traders, as you consider the term, are indeed competing in the stock market, which is not for the faint-hearted. Most stock traders are active risk-takers, making trades after studying the market and gathering whatever information is necessary about a stock or the market. The active risk-taker takes the same approach. They study the market of their purpose (their risk territory) to gather whatever information is necessary to achieve their purpose. As with stock traders, failures happen along the way, but the mindset of the active risk-taker is one of never giving up. They make mistakes, pick themselves up, and keep moving in the direction of their purpose.

The Passive Risk-Taker

The passive risk-taker is a person who takes risks within their level of comfort, or what is commonly referred to as the comfort zone. This level of comfort for the passive risk-taker is usually below what is in the potential of the person or entity and is mainly driven by the fear of loss that may or may not happen if they were to go all in or increase their level of risk appetite. This fear right here is the disease that is holding back about 90% of the people in the world today. Is there anything wrong with being a passive risk-taker? Yes and no. Yes, because knowing that you can achieve a level beyond your current risk appetite and not doing so is selfish. And no, in the sense that no one is going to force you out of your comfort zone as a passive risk-taker. I will leave that for you to think about.

Accidental Risk-Taker

The accidental risk-taker is the person who stumbles upon an opportunity at the right time and takes the risk by taking action to put in the resources—time, money, people, raw material, and so on—to exploit the opportunity and convert it to the desired benefits the opportunity can bring. Time and time again, you have heard the expression 'being at the right place at the right time'. What a perfect condition for bringing your purpose to fruition.

This happened to me in 2018 while on the train into Central London. A guy walked up to take a seat next to me, and in my mind, I thought, *Man, he is a big guy, and it is going to be so tight sitting next to him, which will affect my ability to use my laptop freely.* Nevertheless, I moved over and allowed him to take the aisle seat. I still continued working on my laptop as best I could, and he asked me what I did for work. This question led to a great conversation and to being invited to a private networking event hosted by a renowned coach of top CEOs, who ended up being my coach for a while and continues to mentor me to this day. The lessons I learned through this experience have added so much measurable value to my personal and professional life.

Being an accidental risk-taker is a personality type that means you are always ready to see beyond your immediate self. It is your ability to bring an unknown into a known state where you can measure its value in relation to the purpose driving you.

The Hybrid Risk-Taker

The hybrid risk-taker is the person who shuttles between the active risk-taker and the passive risk-taker personality types. Sometimes, they are active, and other times, they are not, depending on the opportunity. You can compare the hybrid risk-taker to a hybrid vehicle that uses two power sources, electric and petrol, to increase and improve drive efficiency. Each power source can operate independently or collaboratively, depending on the drive mode.

In a similar way, the hybrid risk-taker uses the elements of active and passive risk-taking to achieve their purpose, balanced with a healthy appetite for achieving a level beyond what is typically obtainable if the power sources were operated independently.

Material Risk-Taker

The material risk-taker is a person who takes very high-value or high-stakes risks and whose actions, if negatively impacted, would have a detrimental ripple effect. An example of this can be seen when an influential CEO of a multinational company resigns, negatively impacting the stock market with falling stock prices. Another example is Archduke Franz

Ferdinand of Austria, whose assassination sparked the First World War. Material risk-takers are people in powerful, influential positions or people who take very high risks expecting a high return. You see these in poker games when a material risk-taker is willing to bet all their chips or money to win substantial amounts of money. Of course, there is some fear that they might lose it all, but they are not afraid to go all in because the win will be significant in comparison with the amount invested. That potential outcome is what drives the poker player or, in the case of your purpose, the material risk-taker to go all in.

I am not advocating gambling your life savings away carelessly. You have to know that you are the decider of the future you want, and every risk you take depends on you. The term 'material risk-taker' in banking indicates people whose actions can have a material, significant, or catastrophic impact on the bank. Sometimes in life, you must initiate the material risk-taker personality type. It is the mindset of 'invest big, win big.'

The Dynamic Risk-Taker

The dynamic risk-taker is the person who has the ability to apply all the above-mentioned risk personality types to achieve their purpose. This is the superpower personality type that makes you almost godlike. Dynamism here is indicated by the quality of flexibility, adaptability, fluidity, and 'augmentability' (I just made this word up) to achieve a defined purpose in any given situation. The economy, political climate, geography, and family status do not present obstacles to the achievement of their purpose. Their embodiment of the five risk personality types is executed artistically. This superpower state of being a dynamic risk-taker is acquired with years of consistent risk-taking and testing out all other risk personality types. Sometimes, the dynamic risk-taker is active, passive, accidental, or hybrid. You have to know the drivers that influence your risk-taking ability. You must understand yourself at a deeper psychological level to operate as a dynamic risk-taker.

In quantum physics, dynamism or quantum dynamics refers to how particles, atoms, or suchlike are governed by movement and energy over a period of time. There are three fundamental elements of physics necessary for life in the physical universe: time, space, and matter. They have had to work dynamically to sustain life. In a similar vein, for your purpose to be achieved and sustained, it needs space (the environment where it will materialise), matter (the resources that need to be combined to design, build, and implement it), and it needs time. All these are symbiotically and dynamically needed to achieve your purpose.

CHAPTER TWO

Risk Philosophy and the Psychology of Risk: Building Bridges Over Walls

Philosophy is the accumulation of knowledge to acquire wisdom, while psychology is the application of wisdom to navigate the world in relation to our existence as humans. They go hand in hand.

Risk philosophy, therefore, is the study, understanding, and application of environmental, economic, and social dynamics governing humans in relation to their existence. Risk psychology is the study and understanding of the innate functions of human behaviour and the application of that understanding to navigate the achievement of purpose.

Why is it so important to understand this? Our existence is full of walls—systemic walls and psychological walls—that threaten our ability to take risks and achieve purpose successfully. To overcome these walls or barriers, you need to have the right knowledge and must understand who you are, how you interact with the people around you, and how people interact with you based on the information you project, which identifies who you are at any given time.

By forming your philosophical approach to the world and having an adequate amount of understanding of both yours and others' behavioural responses to environmental triggers, you can overcome the many barriers that will present themselves to you as you pursue your purpose.

Prepare Your Senses for Risk-Taking

It is important for you to know that every great achievement in life or every great feat that has been surmounted involves not just sensory data but, more importantly, far deeper activated senses known as the conscious and unconscious mind or psyche. As taught by the renowned founder of Analytical Psychology, Carl Gustav Jung, the conscious mind or psyche is our field of consciousness, which contains our conscious awareness of the existing and continuing sense of personal identity. It is the organiser of our thoughts and intuitions, feelings, and sensations, and it has access to memories that are not repressed.

In contrast, the unconscious psyche involves the lesser-known activities and workings of the self, which Jung described as:

'Everything of which I know, but of which I am not at the moment thinking; everything of which I was once conscious but have now forgotten; everything perceived by my senses, but not noted by my conscious mind; everything which, involuntarily and without paying attention to it, I feel, think, remember, want, and do; all the future things which are taking shape in me and will sometime come to consciousness; all this is the content of the unconscious.'

(Jung, 1921, *Psychological Types*, Collected Works, Vol. 6)

As I understand it and have experienced it, when the unconscious contents of our psyche break through into consciousness, it can lead to increased levels of development in a person.

Knowing how to use both our conscious and unconscious psyche is essential for taking risks to achieve a purpose, and it is a powerful force for creating success that is in your own hands. Cultures and civilisations have been transformed by this force. Once you know the purpose you want to achieve, you need to commit your senses—both your conscious and unconscious—to it. Know what you know better and understand those internal thoughts and emotions that can work in your favour or against you and your purpose better.

There are three things you can do to bring your senses into alignment for risk-taking.

Thoughts Out Loud

Your thoughts have power in them because they can be the driving force to accomplish great things. From an idea you conceive in your mind to a tangible outcome that impacts millions or billions of people on Planet Earth, if you can see it in your mind, you can hold it in your hand. It all boils down to your level of risk-taking and the related purpose.

From a young age, in elementary school in a village in Nigeria, selling pencils at school during break time, I knew I wanted to run my own business. I did not want to be employed like my father was. Today, I sit here writing this chapter in my own leased office in the United Kingdom where I operate my business, and this is evidence of how far I have come in making my thoughts real. I took risks. Not all of them paid off, but the ones that did certainly propelled me forward in maintaining the course to my purpose. The ones that did not pay off provided knowledge that I reused for continued risk-taking.

Freedom of thought projection is available to everyone. Unfortunately, many repress their own thoughts either out of fear of what the thought would bring to the surface or a deliberate attempt to avoid looking at the person in the mirror. What the mind thinks, it produces. What is the quality of your thought? What your mind thinks is eventually manifested in the quantity equivalent to the value and volume of thoughts thought.

Your thoughts are always present even when they are not experienced. It is like the luggage conveyor belt at the airport terminal. You do not see all the luggage come through at once. They come one after another, some in clusters and others individually, until you see yours and you make a commitment based on how you feel, which makes you go to it and pick it up. In a similar way, thoughts of all sorts are present but not evident until the experience calls for it and it presents itself. It is now down to you to project the thought out loud into reality by taking action directed towards purpose.

It is important to understand this because it influences our decision-making. I will talk about that in the next point. Many people have dormant thoughts, by which I mean thoughts backed by no action—'wishful thinking', as it is often referred to. To achieve success, you do not necessarily have to organise your thoughts in any order; you just need to be clear on a purpose you want to achieve and pick out the thoughts you will act on to help you achieve that purpose. You do not make babies by thinking about it; there are necessary steps involved before you do the deed, and after that, more continued action until the baby is born. It does not end there. You have to take care of the baby until it is grown; otherwise, that purpose can be cut short.

Decision Analysis

Every day, we make decisions about what to eat, what to spend money on, where to live, where to go for date night, and so on. Making decisions is a permanent fixture of life, and the fact is that we make these decisions both consciously and unconsciously. The process of analysing decisions starts before the decision is made and continues after it is made. Such analysis ranges from millisecond analysis to make a lifesaving decision to lengthy analysis to make life-changing decisions. It is a quick decision to jump in the pool to save a child who has just fallen in, but a much slower decision to invest in a life-changing programme. Why? It is because people like these do not have a powerfully motivating purpose that prompts them to take the necessary risks. You allow all sorts of emotions to slow you down and live life passively. Ask yourself: *Do the decisions I make today, as reflected in the things I do daily, align with a worthy and ethical purpose that would benefit others? If you are the CEO or top executive of a company, what drives your decisions? Are the decisions you make adequate and appropriate to achieve the company's purpose?*

I once did a project for a company that was underperforming but had huge potential to be very successful. The executives had no appetite to make the necessary changes to spark growth because their personal purpose did not align with that of the company. They wanted to sell the company for scraps, take their shares and go. I think this is highly unethical because it is the employees who suffer when they are told that they no longer have jobs. The decisions of those at the top, both personal and professional, can have a detrimental impact on the rest of the people that make up that entity. As I mentioned previously, our decisions are influenced by both our conscious and unconscious selves. By bringing them both together, you can make better and more rewarding decisions. Imagine if the impact of every decision you make is worth a pound or a dollar. Incentivise your decisions with some sort of measure, preferably monetary value, and you will stop making decisions that do not pay you.

Risk Linguistic Transference

Language is at the very core of who we are as humans. Unlike animals, we benefit from the gift and ability to form languages and learn to communicate in many languages. Historically, language has played a major role in the expansion of empires. For example, the ancient Roman Empire benefited from linguistic diversity, which enhanced trade and cultural amalgamation, further expanding the empire. At the time of Pentecost (33 C.E.), the Romans ruled over Israel, and there were many people of different languages and cultures there at the time, including Galileans, Cretans (Greeks), Parthians (a tribe in Iran), Medes (today's Azerbaijan), people from Mesopotamia (today's Syria, Turkey, and Iraq), Egypt, Libya, and many more, all living and doing business in Jerusalem. This was around the time when the famous miraculous empowerment to speak in foreign languages was gifted to the disciples of Jesus. It was to enable them to preach the Gospel to this culturally and linguistically diverse group of people so they could advance the message of Christ. This is an indication of the power of language to achieve or advance a purpose. You can read this fascinating story in the book of Acts in the Bible.

What Is Risk Linguistic Transference?

Risk linguistic transference focuses on the arrangement of words to form the language we use to transfer our thoughts and communicate our message while pursuing a specific purpose. It involves the analysis of the thoughts, words, language, and information that we consciously or unconsciously project on the individuals we deal with—our risk subjects, so to speak. It is important to note the three components here: risk, linguistic (or language), and transference (or projection of, to). When combined, it is transformative, enhancing prosperity in purpose, as referenced in the above example of prosperity in Jerusalem under Roman occupation.

- **Risk:** The person or organisation taking action to achieve a defined PURPOSE.
- **Linguistics:** The construction of words to form language that is used to accomplish a PURPOSE.
- **Transference:** The unconscious and conscious projection of information contained in constructed language used by a person or organisation through conscious activities onto their subjects (customers, clients, friends, family, associations) within the PURPOSE.

When using risk linguistic transference, you must be aware of the outcome you want to achieve. Risk linguistic transference will not work on a wild goose chase. You must know the outcome you want from the risk subject (the person). Furthermore, the activities you carry out when using risk linguistic transference must align consistently with the purpose within the defined timeline for the outcome to materialise. You must understand your subject or subjects and their interests by building rapport to avoid creating psychological dissonance, which can break the link in communication, leading to apathy, which then has a knock-on effect on productivity and profitability.

When I developed risk linguistic transference in 2018, I was deeply concerned about the continued negative projection of risk, which always resulted in non-transformative outcomes because the language was incorrectly used. I quickly realised that to change the way risk was perceived and to help people and organisations understand and use the power of transformation and purpose actualisation that risk has to offer, a more powerful approach to speaking about risk needed to be developed. Since then, my involvement in Analytical Psychology has further enhanced this practice, which I am now making available through this book.

Rewire Your Persona for Risk-Taking

Up until this point, it is likely you have tried to achieve several things and have not yet succeeded. It is also probably the first time you are reading a book on how to take risks and achieve your purpose. Congratulations—the investment you made to buy this book and the time you have taken to read it will bring you much closer to achieving your defined purpose. Everything you have done and every piece of knowledge you have needs to be rewired to divert current towards the outcome you want to achieve. It is like driving a car in Nigeria and then relocating to the United Kingdom. If you want to drive legally in the United Kingdom, you need to unlearn all the bad driving habits acquired in an unregulated country. This involves learning the driving codes, taking a theory test, taking several practical driving lessons, and then proceeding to take the practical driving test with an examiner by your side, watching and grading your every move as you execute the test instructions. Well, this was true for me. I passed the driving test on my third attempt and celebrated by giving my driving instructor a bear hug for helping me replace my bad driving habits with good ones and readjust my driving to align with that of the United Kingdom's driving requirements.

The same is true when it comes to conscious risk-taking with a purpose in view. As we go through life, we pick up many ideologies projected onto us through our families, culture, traditions, the school system, the political system, and the commercial or social systems we live in—rarely questioning them. At a foundational level, no one is taught about risk-taking at school. We are not taught how to define our purpose, let alone take steps to achieve it, and that is why the majority of the population in the world ends up coasting through life and doing what everyone around them does when the ability to transcend what is perceived as normal lies within you.

Imagine you are presented with an unattainable lifetime opportunity that would change your life for the better. But to change the reason for its unattainableness, all you have to do is give up the things that limit you from getting this opportunity and acquire the right knowledge and persona that gives you full access to the opportunity. What would you do?

Here are some things you can do to rewire your persona for conscious risk-taking. If you are an organisation, this would be your brand persona, which means the people within your organisation have to have an aligning persona with the brand image you want to project.

- **Build Tolerance for Uncertainty:** Contrary to popular opinions, immense opportunities and rewards exist in uncertainty. So you have to desensitise yourself from the worldview of uncertainty and embrace it by gradually exposing yourself to it without having all the information to give you confidence in it. When you take steps towards uncertainty to find your purpose, then the data will present themselves to you, enabling you to make wise decisions.

- **Surround Yourself with Unlike-minded Risk-Takers:** The saying goes, "You are the average of the five people you surround yourself with." Most people tend to surround themselves with like-minded individuals who keep them comfortable, adding no positive pressure. Break this habit now! Surround yourself with different types of risk-takers, particularly those with high-octane energy, active mindsets, and a dynamic approach to life. They will bring out the potential in you that you never knew you had.

- **Unify Yourself with the Truth:** The most serious lies you can tell are the lies you tell yourself. Examine the depth of your personal unconscious, the part of you that you do not share with anyone else, to understand the seat of your motivations. When you have accessed your unconscious mind, stay there for a bit and have an honest conversation with it. Does it align with the purpose that you want to achieve?

- **Be Mindful:** Being mindful means being aware of the elements that are not immediately accessible to your consciousness but can influence your thoughts, feelings and behaviour. Your duty is to identify these and integrate them so that you can become whole within yourself, giving you the tools to take risks consciously and achieve the purpose you want. This is also essential for organisations but may be more complex to attain due to the number of people within. This can be achieved using active imagination exercises delivered through training, coaching, and various types of cues to create a unified entity that serves and delivers its purpose.

- **Practice Visualisation:** Visualisation is a psychological technique that involves creating mental pictures or scenarios in your mind. It is used in various contexts, such as business, sports, therapy, education, and self-improvement, to enhance performance, reduce stress, or achieve specific goals. This is an essential part of risk and risk-taking because it allows you to explore both positive and negative scenarios and decide the best course of action to take towards achieving your purpose. Visualisation techniques strengthen your connection with your purpose. For organisations and brands, this goes beyond simply outlining your vision and posting it on your website. From the top to the lower levels of your organisation, you need to use visualisation techniques to align the activities being performed with your purpose.

Rewiring your persona for risk-taking involves a combination of mindset changes, behavioural changes, and progressive exposure to risk-taking. By building resilience, embracing uncertainty, and developing confidence in your decision-making abilities, you can become more comfortable with taking risks and increase your chances of achieving success in various areas of life.

The Need to Rewire Your Persona for Risk-Taking

The world is changing rapidly. Imagine this for a second: Let us say you have defined a purpose today that you would like to achieve in five years. If you did everything the same way as you did on day one for the next five years, what do you think would happen to that purpose? It is highly likely you would not achieve the purpose. It is like a house that was built a hundred years ago. To conform with electrical standards, it would need to be rewired to some extent, with some elements changed for the house to be powered sufficiently.

Similarly, to take risks successfully, you have to move with the times. The methods I mentioned above on how you can rewire your persona for risk-taking are a continuous process. In addition, you must update your thinking and adapt your thoughts, knowledge, and actions to enable you to navigate the changing world. This is necessary for personal, professional, and organisational growth along with adaptability in times of local or global shifts (which may involve external factors beyond our control) and, most importantly, resilience in times of stress (which may include crises of any sort). The ability to adapt and take risks successfully is crucial because the world is in constant motion. Staying abreast ensures that you remain dynamic and can capitalise on new opportunities and address threats and problems effectively.

Embrace Difference

Fear creates paralysis in risk-taking. The sensory faculties needed to propel you to take risks require you to do things others would not do, which is why so many people are cocooned together in the cosy comforts of systemic cycles, like a merry-go-round in the circus of life. Get it together now! You will not achieve your purpose in this state because, eventually, you get glued to the people you are cosied up to and will not stand up to stand out for you to be seen and heard. If you are not seen and heard, then how relevant are you?

Embracing difference means that you must develop yourself to become individuated from societal constructs. It is a state where you have been formed out of your own conscious actions and are aware of your unconscious psyche, guiding it to be an integral part of who you are. This involves diverging from collective norms, general expectations, and stereotypes to become your true self. Fear of social rejection, fear of failure, and cultural formations are some of the common factors that make it difficult for some individuals to embrace being different, thus falling short of the rewards that come from being purposefully different.

In my first book, *For the Love of Purpose: Take These 7 Steps to Achieve Your Purpose*, in 'Step 3: Educate Yourself the Right Way', I talked about the value of education, but not just education within the four walls of an academic institution—that will only keep you in the status quo. You need to go beyond that to acquire the wisdom that enables you to understand how the world really works. This acquisition of uncommon knowledge is what will set you apart and empower you to create wealth, build resilience, and confront the fears others run away from.

Understanding the Spiritual Forces of Risk

It is virtually unknown to anyone that risk has its own spirits, or shall we say 'forces' that it transmits when it impacts its subjects. It is like a mosquito with the malaria virus it possesses. When it bites you, it transmits the malaria disease. I just had to use this illustration, having been bitten too many times and had malaria a few times when I lived in Nigeria. To be successful in the achievement of any purpose, you need to understand the spirits each variant of risk possesses and be able to manoeuvre them according to their kind. It is a case of the good, the bad, and the ugly spirits with risk. Just pray for the good one to find you.

To illustrate further, threats bring a certain kind of force that is felt by the recipient that opportunities do not bring because opportunities possess their own unique force.

What I am saying is that each variant of risk—threats, problems, opportunities, and rewards—has its own unique spirit peculiar to it. When threats to a purpose present themselves, the spirit or force of the threat is projected onto the owner or subjects connected to the purpose. It is the same thing with problems, opportunities, and rewards. Each of these variants of risk affects its subjects; it possesses the recipients of each variant of risk differently. It sounds like a horror movie, depending on which variant affects you, but there is a happy ending.

Let us test this out for a second. How would you feel if you were threatened by the possibility of losing your home? How would you feel if threatened by the possibility of losing your job? How would you feel if threatened by the possibility of a loved one dying due to age or sickness? You probably felt something inside of you as you read these potential scenarios. What you felt is a projection of the forces or spirit that threats bring with them. Not a good one.

Now, counter these scenarios with the reward variant of risk. How do you feel when you pass a job interview and secure a new job after being jobless for a while? How would you feel if you had lost everything you had and someone handed you an envelope with a cheque for £100,000, accompanied by a letter saying, 'This is my gift to you'? How would you feel if you just had your first child after trying for many years to have a baby? The feelings you had were more positive than the former scenarios. The thing is that you cannot substitute these forces. You cannot cheat them. They are what they are, and they will possess you with what they bring at one time or another in life and your journey to any purpose you are seeking to achieve.

What I have just revealed to you is the wisdom that gives you mastery over the dynamic forces that influence your purpose, whatever the purpose is. It is imperative that you know this and understand how to work with the spiritual forces of risk because your success, your life, and the lives of the people associated with your purpose depend on the relationship you have with these forces and your ability to move them in flows according to their kind to create the outcome you want.

You almost want to be like a football club manager. The person that comes to my mind is Jose Mourinho, former Chelsea Football Club manager. His purpose was for the club to be number one in the Premiership. He knows the strengths of each player in each game. He places each player in their power position to be able to win the game. The manager knows each player but has a different kind of relationship with each player. What separates the football club manager from the player is his ability to see a much wider view of the purpose, from players' health, administration, training, and much more. The players almost have a singular view, which is to score and win the game. You have to have a different type of relationship with each risk variant and move them according to their powers to achieve your purpose.

Archetypal Influences in Risk

In my study of psychology, I learned about archetypes, and I had an unveiling of sorts about how underlying human factors, referred to as the 'unconscious', affect several aspects of our lives and everything we do. It is when you start to learn deeply that manifestations of the realities present make themselves apparent to you. This realisation opened up a new understanding to me of how deeply ingrained patterns of behaviour influence our decisions, particularly when it comes to taking risks, whether as individual persons or in a collective sense as corporate entities. Risk, it turns out, is not just a matter of chance but is deeply connected to ancient patterns of behaviour passed down to us genetically. In a collective sense, referring to corporate entities, organisations or societies, this is often missed, not understood and may account for integration issues on several levels that lead to corporate catastrophes.

Archetypes, as defined in Jungian psychology, are universal symbols or messages that reside in our minds as a part of the psyche that holds the memories and experiences of humanity as a whole. These memories are not personal but shared across all people, forming the basis for the archetypes. Jung believed that these archetypes are inherited and manifest in our dreams, myths, and even daily behaviours.

To put it simply, an archetype is like a blueprint for the way humans typically respond to certain situations. For example, the Hero is a common archetype representing courage, strength, and perseverance in the face of adversity. The Shadow, another archetype, embodies the darker aspects of our personality, the things we might prefer to keep hidden from others and even from ourselves.

When it comes to risk, several archetypes come into play, shaping how we perceive and respond to uncertainty. One of the most influential is the **Trickster**. The Trickster is often depicted as a figure who disrupts the status quo, challenges norms, and takes risks that others might shy away from. This archetype can be seen in many cultures, from the Nigerian Igbo land, Mbe the Tortoise to the Native American Coyote. The Trickster's influence in our lives can push us to take risks, sometimes for the better and sometimes leading us into chaotic situations. Personally, I believe this archetype is not just influential but also one of the most important because of its powerful ability to bring about change in deeply entrenched ideologies or systems. Take for example, the Tortoise archetype in the Igbo culture (a central character in many Igbo folktales), which is often portrayed as cunning, resourceful, and deceitful. Despite his slow and unassuming appearance, Mbe uses his intelligence and trickery to outwit other animals, including those who are physically stronger or more powerful. The same is true of the Native American Coyote archetype, which is said to be multifaceted, embodying both foolishness and wisdom, chaos and creation, humour and danger. Three real-life examples of the trickster archetype I would site are:

1. Nina Simone, the legendary singer, songwriter, and civil rights activist, exemplified the trickster archetype in her fearless approach to challenging racial and social injustices. Through her music and public statements, she often confronted and subverted the expectations of the time, using her platform to deliver powerful messages that were both provocative and transformative. Songs like "Mississippi Goddam" and "Four Women" served as pointed critiques of racism and inequality. Simone's legacy as a trailblazer in both music and social activism continues to influence and inspire, demonstrating the power of the trickster archetype in challenging the status quo.

2. Elon Musk, the entrepreneur behind companies like Tesla and SpaceX, often displays trickster qualities through his unconventional ideas, bold challenges to established industries, and unpredictable public behaviour, particularly on social media. Musk frequently subverts traditional business practices and norms, using his charisma and innovation to push boundaries in technology and space exploration. His tweets and public statements, often provocative and controversial, further align him with the trickster archetype. Musk's influence on technology and business is profound,

and his trickster-like approach has led to significant disruptions in various industries, from automotive to space travel.

3. Donald Trump, the 45th President of the United States and real estate mogul, is a classic modern-day trickster figure. His approach to politics and business has been marked by a consistent subversion of norms, unpredictability, and a flair for manipulation and showmanship. Trump frequently challenged and upended established political and social conventions, using unorthodox methods to communicate and govern, such as his prolific use of Twitter before being banned from it and his unfiltered public statements. The typical trickster archetype saw him launch his alternative to Twitter (now X), Truth Social, which he now uses as his own platform. His ability to manipulate media narratives, often by disseminating controversial information, is a classic trickster tactic, keeping both supporters and detractors constantly engaged and reactive. Trump's influence has been transformative in many ways, particularly in reshaping the Republican Party and altering the norms of American political discourse. His trickster-like disruption has led to significant shifts in political alliances. His presidency and public persona have sparked ongoing debates about truth, governance, and the power of charisma in leadership, making him one of the most polarising and impactful figures in recent history.

Another important archetype in the context of risk is the **Hero**. The Hero's journey often involves taking risks, facing challenges, and overcoming obstacles. This archetype inspires us to be brave, to step out of our comfort zones, and to pursue goals that seem daunting. However, the Hero can also lead us into risky situations, driven by the belief that we must conquer or achieve something great, sometimes at a significant personal cost.

The **Caregiver** is another archetype that influences our relationship with risk. This archetype is driven by a desire to protect and nurture others. In terms of risk, the Caregiver might be more of a passive risk-taker, being more cautious producing failure for others or themselves. This cautious approach can be beneficial, but it can also prevent us from seizing opportunities that require a leap of faith into uncertainty where opportunities may be present.

The interplay of these archetypes can be seen in everyday decisions, from career choices to personal relationships. For instance, someone influenced by the Hero archetype might choose to start a high-risk business, driven by the need to prove themselves and achieve something significant. In contrast, another person, guided by the Caregiver archetype, might choose a safer, more stable career path to ensure the well-being of their family earning a salary.

Understanding these archetypal influences can help us recognise why we approach risk the way we do. It allows us to see that our decisions are not just random or purely logical but are shaped by deeper, often unconscious patterns. By becoming aware of these influences, understanding these ancient patterns, we gain insight into our behaviours and motivations, allowing us to navigate the uncertainties of life with greater wisdom and awareness so we can make more informed choices and be on the right path to achieve our intended purpose.

CHAPTER THREE

The Seven Essential Rules of Risk

The power of risk is that it gives you access to everything. But to gain the benefits of that power, there are rules you must follow. These rules force you to operate at a higher level, enabling you to achieve beyond what is commonly accepted. This is what creates the significantly influential, powerful, and most successful few people on earth who create their own economies and are not threatened by what happens on the global economic landscape.

Let us look at the first rule and work our way down to the seventh rule to see how you can empower yourself to build unfathomable resilience in the face of world events.

Rule One: Define Your Purpose

This is the most powerful rule. Without a defined purpose, you will be chasing after the wind, and your power will become weak. Think about this: Humans for centuries have consistently asked themselves one question: *Why are we here?* We want to know why the Earth is the only home known for life. We want to know why we grow old and die even though we have a limitless brain capacity that can carry and process immense amounts of data for millions of years to come. 'Why' is a fundamental aspect of risk, and that is the reason I define risk as a person or an entity with a purpose, linking risk to the fundamental question of existence. You cannot take risks successfully without a clearly defined purpose. In my first book, *For the Love of Purpose: Take These 7 Steps To Achieve Your Purpose*, I described the importance of having a clearly defined purpose and how you can achieve it. I recommend you get that book because it goes into detail on the essentials of purpose, as it is the foundation of everything you want to achieve in life.

To define your purpose, you need to formulate the problem you want to solve for yourself and others. In this purpose formulation, a mission statement would emerge that describes the objective of you, a brand, a business, or an organisation. Let us look at some examples of purpose definitions:

1. **Google:** To organise the world's information and make it universally accessible and useful.

2. **Shell:** Power progresses together by providing more and cleaner energy solutions.

3. **Nike:** To bring inspiration and innovation to every athlete in the world.

4. **Bank of America:** To help make financial lives better through the power of every connection.

5. **Walt Disney:** To entertain, inform, and inspire people around the globe through the power of unparalleled storytelling, reflecting the iconic brands, creative minds, and innovative technologies that make ours the world's premier entertainment company.

6. **PricewaterhouseCoopers (PwC):** To build trust in society and solve important problems.

These clearly defined purposes show you how powerful having a defined purpose is, as evidenced by these industry giants and the successes they have and continue to accumulate. PwC took this a notch up and has even hired a Head of Purpose. What a statement there! I think every organisation needs a Head of Purpose.

Consider the way these purposes are structured. There is an outcome; they indicate the problems being solved and, more importantly, drive the development of opportunities, converting them into solutions that provide benefits while dynamically managing threats. When you give birth to a purpose, the risk begins and ends with that purpose.

Rule Two: Develop the Vision for Your Purpose

Your vision is the channel by which your purpose is achieved. It is a representation of your purpose in a materialised state. Your vision is one of the supporting pillars of your purpose. You cannot have one without the other.

Visualisation involves seeing what that purpose is, what it is doing in the future, what it is going to achieve, and who it is going to impact. You want to almost feel the impact of your purpose now. It is like watching a television programme—you are visualising an activity in the present even though it may have been pre-recorded and having a real-time sensory response to it, which may or may not satisfy a desire. Visualisation is important because it means that in your mind's eye, you are always going to be seeing your purpose. You are going to be living it in the present, even though it is in the future. That is important. Most companies, when they define their businesses or their organisations, have a vision statement. A vision statement is what you say you aim to achieve. This is directly related to your purpose. Many companies, when they define their businesses or set out their vision, tend to miss out on the purpose. Only more recently have companies started thinking about purpose. There has been a transformation in how companies are seeking to be established. Because without purpose, it is going to be difficult to take the risks you seek to get there. Your vision is the channel by which your purpose is achieved. It is a representation of your purpose in a materialised state.

Your vision is one of the supporting pillars of your purpose. You cannot have one without the other.

To develop your vision, you need the following things:

1. Know the purpose that is to be achieved.
2. Create the channel by which the purpose will be achieved.
3. Establish your core values.
4. Envision the change that will come from the purpose.
5. Visualise the outcome of the change.
6. Draft the vision statement that supports your purpose.

Here is a good example of a vision statement aligned with a defined purpose from Google:

1. **Purpose:** To organise the world's information and make it universally accessible and useful.
2. **Vision:** Providing access to the world's information in one click.

You can see how both the purpose and vision work in alignment.

Visualising the purpose you seek is essential. This means that everyone else—not just you, the business owner, or the CEO of the company, but everyone else in the business or organisation—needs to embody the vision. They need to see this vision and buy into it. When people do not buy into the vision, it creates disunity within the organisation. Many employees will suffer from low morale. Those in the business who do not buy into the vision are just there for the money, making money for themselves. Most of them may become bottlenecks in terms of achieving your purpose. Everyone within the business needs to know the purpose and the vision that the company is seeking to achieve. Because they are also on this path, they need to be taking the risks as well. It is not just the business owner, the CEO, or the C-level executives—everyone within the business needs to be ready for risk-taking because risk-taking is essential for achieving the purpose of the business. Always remember to reiterate the purpose and the vision to your team regularly.

It is essential that people are reminded of the vision. When employees come to work, they want to be aligned with that vision. You also want to make sure that when you choose people who are going to be part of the journey or come with you on this risk-taking path to achieve your purpose, they too are personally and professionally aligned with the purpose and, without a doubt, with the vision.

Rule Three: Create the Roadmap for Your Purpose

Following rule two, you now want to start planning out your roadmap, which should be a lot clearer after you have completed the exercises of the first two rules. Road-mapping the journey means you have to have a scheme for your risk-taking. Remember, you have the purpose, and the activities involved in achieving that purpose constitute your risk-taking. But to get there, you need a map. That is what I call road mapping.

Let us say, for example, we want to start a watch dealership business selling mid-range watches online with the goal of earning £500,000 in twelve months. You would need to build a 12-month roadmap that outlines the amount of sales and activities required to achieve that. By dividing the twelve-month roadmap into four quarters: Q1 (months one to three), Q2 (months four to six), Q3 (months seven to nine), and Q4 (months ten to twelve), you can set goals, targets, and milestones that hold you accountable to the purpose you want to achieve. Of course, this should be supported by your own drive and commitment. What this does is drive attention, effort, and resources towards achieving the purpose of the watch brand in the example. At the start of your roadmap, you need to ensure it is aligned with the purpose you want to achieve by deciding what the associated goals are for each section of the roadmap.

This is where a lot of people get things wrong. Most people talk about achieving goals, but the most important thing they forget is that the goals need to 'live' within a purpose. You cannot achieve a purpose without goals. If you are setting goals that are not aligned with a purpose, then you are limiting your ability to achieve the full potential that is possible.

According to several studies, one carried out by the University of Scranton, Pennsylvania, USA, led by Dr John C. Norcross and published in the Journal of Clinical Psychology in 2002, only 92% were successful in achieving their goals. A more recent article by McKinsey & Company, the world-famed consultancy, written in January 2024, discussed the common pitfalls in goal setting within organisations, reinforcing that effective goal-setting practices are crucial for success.

None of these studies mentioned anything about aligning your goals to a defined purpose, which is why the ratio of success in goal-setting alone remains high. You must define your purpose first, then align the goals to it and use your roadmap to navigate to the purpose.

The following diagram shows you how a roadmap should work.

12 Month Roadmap				
Milestones	Q1	Q2	Q3	Q4
Goals	£100,000	£200,000	£300,000	£510,000
Targets (Services or goods costing £1000 per unit)	Sell **50** Units a month	Sell **70** Units a month	Sell **105** Units a month	Sell **180** Units a month
Tasks (Daily activities that need to be performed to achieve a purpose)	Increase sales calls to **200** a day and other associated tasks	Increase sales calls to **250** a day and other associated tasks	Increase sales calls to **300** a day and other associated tasks	Increase sales calls to **350** a day and other associated tasks

Current State/ Defined Purpose — Future State/ Achieved Purpose

Figure 2. Purpose Roadmap: Example of how a roadmap should work

Rule Four: Assemble Your Purpose Warriors

Your purpose warriors are the like-minded risk-takers you assemble to go after the purpose you want to achieve. It is often said that a house divided against itself will not stand. Infighting among executive board members, executive coups, personality clashes, and uncontrolled egos are just a few of the factors commonly responsible for slowing down the achievement of an organisation's purpose, astronomical financial losses, or the eventual collapse of a once powerful and successful organisation. Lehman Brothers is a very good example, and its collapse is often cited as a critical trigger that exacerbated the financial crisis of 2008. In his book, *A Colossal Failure of Common Sense: The Inside Story of the Collapse of Lehman Brothers*, Larry McDonald, author and former employee of Lehman Brothers, revealed the extent of disunity amongst the members of the Executive Committee and their respective stakeholders, which exacerbated the avoidable collapse of the bank. Opportunities to avert the crisis were there but not taken. One of the lines in the book that resonates strongly was, 'If only the reign of terror that drove out the most brilliant of Lehman's traders and risk takers had been halted earlier...'

To ensure your risk-taking leads to your purpose being achieved and expanded, you need people you can rely on. In my experience, it hurts you whenever you hire, work, or collaborate with people who do not value the purpose you want to achieve as much as you do, often resulting in having to fire employees, partners, and consultants. Most people will associate themselves with you for their own interests. They are not your purpose warriors. You need like-minded warriors who are going to stay the course, whatever it takes.

I listened to a podcast a little while back featuring Scott Shay, founder of Signature Bank, who was at the time also its CEO. It highlighted the importance of hiring people who are more experienced than you are. What struck me was his approach to assembling his purpose warriors. He said that if he had not hired 'Joseph J. DePaolo and John Tamberlane, there would not have been a Signature Bank today'. Signature Bank was the only bank in the US that did not require a government bailout during the 2008 financial crisis due to its stability. He cites having the right partners as an important factor in achieving success. This is because you can recover from almost anything in business except for having the wrong partners. Having the wrong partners or purpose warriors could mean the death of your purpose.

What I learned from Scott in this podcast is that you have to have a reasonable amount of 'courtship' period with the people you want to bring on board to work with you on your purpose, especially those who are your core team or top team. I recommend listening to this podcast, which you can find on Spotify. Unfortunately, in 2023, a few years after Scott Shay left the bank, Signature Bank collapsed due to systemic failures, which, if I am not mistaken, resulted from the wrong people at the helm who were not aligned with its original purpose.

Rule Five: See Opportunity in Everything Until Proven Otherwise

Everything is an opportunity waiting to be exploited for its rewards, including what is perceived as failure. It is your duty to access and assess these opportunities and then make the decisions on which opportunities you want to exploit. When you accept failure, it means you have been defeated by an opportunity that presented itself to you because you have not given the opportunity, which appeared in the form of failure, the right amount of effort or used the tool specifically appropriate for the opportunity to deliver the reward. Methods vary; you cannot use the method for opportunity A to exploit opportunity B, just as a farmer cannot use a hoe to milk a cow.

Note that there is a difference between accepting failure and acknowledging failure. When you accept failure, it means you have given up on the opportunity that appeared as a failure. When you acknowledge failure, it means you see beyond the perceived failure, take the perceived failure as a stress test, and rework your approach to exploiting the opportunity until you get the results you want. Do not make the mistake of seeking out one opportunity, as most people do, or waiting for 'that big singular break'. You need multiple opportunities because even if one opportunity is successful, it is not sufficient to achieve the purpose you want to achieve or to keep it. Untapped opportunities in the billions if not trillions due to the traditional practice of risk management as risk

The very nature of this risk variant, opportunity, indicates that it carries a certain potential quantifiable value that warrants us to take the necessary steps, appropriate action, and act promptly. As it is often said, 'Opportunity waits for no one'.

Rule Six: Understand How the World Works in Relation to Your Purpose

This is one rule that must not be taken for granted. So many people wonder why certain things do not work out for them, and this might just be the reason why. Understanding how the world works in relation to your purpose gives you the ability to navigate your approach to your purpose.

To demonstrate, would you take the risk of travelling to a country you have never been to before without first understanding how to get there? Among other things, you would want to find out how you would get around, what currency is used there, are there any safety issues, what language is spoken, and so on, so that you can successfully achieve the purpose of your travel, whether it is for holiday, adventure, or business. The same can be said when you take risks to achieve a life or business purpose. There are fundamental things you need to do in relation to the environment where your risk-taking will happen and where your purpose will be operating or serving you and the intended subjects. Here are some questions you would need to answer to help you understand the world in relation to your purpose:

- What are the potential challenges and obstacles to my purpose?
- How will existing power structures and institutions influence my purpose?
- Who is the penholder/decision-maker I need to work with or partner with?
- What laws or regulations do I need to comply with?
- Where can I get more essential information that others are not privy to and can significantly bring value?
- How prepared am I to adapt to radical systemic changes? (we will discuss resilience in Chapter Eight)

Once your purpose is defined, the visualisation process should encapsulate the information you gather as part of understanding the world dynamics in relation to your purpose.

Rule Seven: Increase Risk-Taking

For growth to happen, you have to increase your level of risk-taking. It is the law of growth, the law of physics, and the law of life. An astronaut cannot ascend into outer space with an aeroplane because it does not have the same level of thrust a rocket has. To achieve your future purpose, you must put yourself in situations that force you to operate at a level higher than where you currently are because the closer you get to your purpose, the harder it gets financially, psychologically, mentally, emotionally and physically. If loss occurs when you are close to your purpose, it is because you failed to maintain momentum with commensurate actions. Your loss will be critical, the pain greater, and the cost higher. But you must have a higher personal and pain tolerance to overcome the loss and continue to your purpose. SpaceX had seven near-death experiences before it achieved its purpose. A progressive increase in risk-taking requires that you persevere in periods of intense pressure, thereby building a higher level of resilience, capability, and capacity to achieve your purpose.

I often get criticised and challenged by the risk management community for urging people to focus on risk exploitation because that is where all your money is. Focusing on just managing risk takes money away from you; risk exploitation driven by the right risk-taking puts money in your pocket. It is impossible to manage what you do not have. First, you have to 'take', then manage what you have 'taken', and continue to increase your 'takings' with what you have until you achieve your purpose.

I recommend following these rules in the order that I have laid out for the best results. At the very least, you must follow rules one, two, and three to establish a solid foundation for your risk-taking activities.

CHAPTER FOUR

Risk Territory Map

Territorial behaviour is present in almost every living thing: dogs, cats, monkeys, and so on. In the first few months of bringing my daughter's cat, Lola, home, it was territorial warfare over who ruled the home. Lola would mark territory by scratching furniture and peeing in certain corners of the house despite having a clean litter box, and then there was the 'eyeballing'. I figured out what 'eyeballing' meant: If I made eye contact with her, she stayed put, but the minute I turned my back, there she was, going where she was not meant to go. Like lightning, she was in the kitchen sink or under the beds. I think we got that sorted out and now know who the boss is, but she still tries me occasionally.

What this cat behaviour shows is that it is innate within mammals and humans alike to carve out a little corner of the world that we can call our own. But what is most common is that most people limit this to where they live and work. In Nigeria, where I spent most of my youth, a common term used by people who want to get a portion of the resources the country has to offer is 'National Cake.' This 'National Cake' represents multiple opportunities, such as crude oil, minerals, precious stones, and government contracts—highly rewarding opportunities present in the country, waiting to be taken by people in government or citizens alike by hook or by crook—often depending on having the right connections. Opportunities are in abundance in whatever country you live in, but we have a problem with disequilibrium in spread, not allocation. I say 'spread' because no one is going to allocate opportunities to you. You have to find them, create them, and convert them to what pays you. For this, you need your risk territory map because, if you do not, you will not access the opportunities you need to feed your family or will be overpowered by the more powerful or more crooked, who take more than they should, leaving many in poverty.

Your risk territory map is a representation of where your opportunities are on the global map. It is not limited to where you live and does not necessarily mean you have to relocate to another country. Rather, it is your method of exploring and unearthing your opportunities through the use of a well-scoped risk territory map.

The best way I can illustrate this is with a board game you might be familiar with called Risk. The aim of the board game is world domination. Players compete to capture territories on a world map (risk territory map), using armies to attack, defend, and conquer. The game involves strategy, negotiation, and chance (through the rolling of dice). Players attempt to conquer territories, form alliances, and eliminate their opponents' armies to eventually control the entire map. The winner is the player who succeeds in conquering all territories on the board.

You are a player in this board game of life, and you are either being played or you are an active player on the global risk territory map. Understandably, world domination may not be your quest, but for you to know your place on the global risk territory map, you need your own risk territory map to give your purpose clear direction.

Why You Need a Risk Territory Map

McKinsey & Company, Klynveld Peat Marwick Goerdeler (KPMG), PricewaterhouseCoopers (PwC), and Deloitte are just a few of the global management consultancy companies with dominance that have strategically drawn up their risk territory map on a global scale. These companies know where their opportunities are because they have explored the regions on their risk territory map by putting boots on the ground and being tasked with locating and then exploiting opportunities. It is worth noting that when these companies started, they may have begun with one person and then grew beyond their place and person of origin. The key people running these companies see that they can extend their map and access opportunities that government organisations cannot, which is why they have a close relationship with most governments of the world. That relationship is so close that many government officials go to work or consult for these management companies when they leave office, giving them continued access to untapped or unexploited opportunities that may have been overlooked or that they do not have the ability to unearth by themselves. What I have demonstrated here is how powerful organisations use these maps for their expansion into billions or trillions of dollars in revenue. This is the sole reason why you need your risk territory map.

In 1992, when I studied Geography for a bachelor's degree at Abia State University in Nigeria, one of the important modules I loved was Cartography (the study of the creation and use of maps). What I learned, which I surprisingly still remember, was the reason for the creation of maps. Map design and creation are vital for the economic expansion of any society. A cartographer is a person who designs and creates maps. They typically work for government agencies, military and defence, consulting companies, or in technology.

None of these organisations would exist today or have a far-reaching effect on the world stage if they did not have the maps they use, created by cartographers, to explore and exploit opportunities. When you think of the work cartographers do to create regional or national maps, you probably now know how important creating your risk territory map is. Having a mental map of your opportunities is great, but consciously designing it, developing it, and knowing where the 'opportunity resources' are can be exceptionally rewarding. Some of the prework you need to undertake for your risk territory map includes, but is not limited to, data collection about the opportunity and its potential, interpreting data, communicating with many people in varying roles, and so on. Doing this exposes the nature of the identified opportunities you want to explore and exploit, but you have to draw the map by better carrying out the activities required for exploration and exploitation.

Charting the Pathway for Expansion

In the ancient Roman era, when nations wanted to go into battle, they did not just send the military out with no clear purpose. The military mapped out the territory it wanted to conquer, incorporating tough terrains, where they were likely to have more casualties, and where the booty was, such as gold, silver, livestock, or land. In most cases, it was the conquest of lands for territorial expansion. That is how most nations expanded. From a personal perspective, we are naturally made to expand—biologically through procreation and growth. Mentally, we grow through brain elasticity, which is required to operate in the real world in a way that a baby cannot. Expansion is in our nature, and it is essential to consciously go through life with not just a desire but also a conscious act of expansion.

Unfortunately, most of the world is governed systematically by national frameworks that have wired many of us to work against our instinct for natural individual expansion. Rather, we follow a construct within the map that has been designed by centuries-old European leaders and very powerful merchants, run as a playbook (or map) for most countries of the world today, which continues to yield wealth for the Anglo-American world power and its allies. Although China and Russia are now threatening this, as these two nations are currently embarking on the modern-day 'Scramble for Africa', what is consistent here is the use of a map for these national expansions.

It was not odd to find terrestrial globe maps in the studies of influential people and great merchants going back as far as the second century A.D. by

Greek philosopher and geographer Crates of Mallus. Martin Behaim, a German mapmaker, navigator, and merchant, made a terrestrial globe map called the Erdapfel, which was a representation of the world pre-Christopher Columbus's voyage. This map featured information from Marco Polo, who travelled to the famous Silk Road in the thirteenth century as a merchant. These little historical facts are significant because they show that these maps were not just geographical tools but exploration and exploitation tools.

Our desire for expansion is evidence that we want more than what we have been permitted to have through these national frameworks, which funnel huge benefits to those who have the ability and willpower to acquire obscene amounts of wealth. To create somewhat of an equilibrium, each person must increase their risk-taking through exploration and exploitation of opportunities and be willing to experience the pressure that expansion creates in them physically, emotionally, and mentally for it to produce its results. For your self-fulfilling prophecy as defined in your purpose to come true, you need a dynamic map coupled with high-intensity risk-taking to elevate yourself or your entity above where you are now.

Strategic Imperatives for a Risk Territory Map

Many factors demand that you have a risk territory map: the rising cost of living, inflation, family expansion, geopolitical tensions, and the list goes on. Having your risk territory map gives you confidence and empowers you because you have almost 100% immunity from the tensions of the world when factors outside your control cause a shockwave. When this happens, you want to maintain a trajectory of growth, knowing where your opportunities are. Most people think that opportunities disappear in times of crisis. This is far from the truth! When crises occur, most opportunities flow to beneficiaries who exploit the situation at hand—whether it is a pandemic, warfare, or a cyber-attack that shuts down a major infrastructure, just like in the movie

Leave the World Behind with Julia Roberts. (Shout out to Eden for getting me to watch the movie.)

Cyber-attacks, wars, pandemics—whatever the crisis, someone is benefitting. While fear and uncertainty grip the populace, forcing them to give up on their pursuits or unmapped opportunities, someone else is busy gathering them for their advantage. It is almost like when people run away from their homes during a conflict, leaving valuables behind. Those who take high risks, mostly the soldiers or warring nations, take the bounties of war. It happened in ancient times, and it happens today. The Russian–US–China push and pull is a great prophetic example. Understanding how the world works will enable you to master the frequencies on which opportunities flow.

Mastering this requires the elevation of thought levels above the level of the worker bee movement. It involves knowing the key players in the world and what they do because they are the ones that create global systemic shocks that bring about the changes that seem to govern the way most of the world lives. When these key players *'flap their wings in the United States, a forest fire starts in Africa, somewhere in the Middle East, and Central and South America'*. These key players, often represented by their organisations and dynamic systems, operate on the basis of how our interconnected societies function as designed if everyone herds in the direction they pull. When you take the time to study these systems, you find opportunities in places others do not, and you become almost immune to systemic shocks.

It is hard to believe that opportunities abound in periods of inflation, increased cost of living, health crises, warfare, environmental disasters, and social crises, but they do. The question is, who benefits where others lose? These events are imperatives for a risk territory map because this is how those who benefit thrive, whereas others operate at an average or below-average level or completely lose out, dying either figuratively or literally.

How to Create Your Risk Territory Map

Around the first week of December 2017, I was reading a book at Bogota Coffee, my favourite coffee shop in Milton Keynes. A man with a full grey beard walked up to me and, showing me his phone, asked, 'How do you like this picture of you?' I was puzzled and at the same time pleased that someone saw me at that precise moment, took note of me and took a picture of me without my knowing. Apparently, my posture at the time, along with the lighting from the angle I sat, was a photographic moment not to be missed— an opportunity. It turns out he has a photography hobby and a penchant for capturing significant moments. What was more significant was that he was a very high-ranking naval officer in the Kuwaiti Navy at the time who was visiting the United Kingdom. We sat talking, and after four hours of sitting there with him, I had received a lesson in military strategies and their parallels in business. That was an invaluable opportunity I took advantage of by giving it my time. I presented the condition for me to receive that lesson and to build that relationship, which I still have to this day. If, by my attitude, I had reacted negatively by being offended as to why a stranger took my photo without my permission, I would not have received the lecture I did at that coffee shop from a phenomenal person like him, nor would I have the opportunity to share some of that with you in this section.

(Photo credit: CDRE(R) Ahmad Alkandri, PhD MSc BEng)

Me and Ahmad

(Photo credit: CDRE[R] Ahmad Alkandri, PhD MSc BEng)

There are so many things I learned from this experience, and I will articulate some of the information I got, giving you my interpretation of what you need to create your risk territory map before you begin your journey to achieving your purpose or augmenting an existing one. I will show you the specific military strategies and how to apply them personally and professionally to any purpose you want to achieve. As you go through this, imagine what this will look like with the characters and the territory of the purpose you are working on achieving. Draw it out on paper so you can bring it to life, and at the end, look at what you have drawn out, just like a military commander looks at a territory map before going into battle. You are the general of your purpose, so let us get to work.

1. **Purpose Clarity**
   a. **Military Strategy:** This strategy focuses on having a clearly defined purpose for going into warfare. Knowing the mission's outcome allows for focused strategy and resource allocation.
   b. **Personal and Professional (Business) Application:** Define your purpose clearly, with incentivised goals. Visualise the outcome you want to achieve in varying stages, recognising that these successes are what will lead you to your purpose, whether it is revenue, assets, reputation or leadership status.

2. **The Principle of Surprise**
   a. **Military Strategy:** This involves attacking at an unexpected time or place, using unconventional tactics, or employing new technology that the enemy is unprepared to counter.
   b. **Personal and Professional (Business) Application:** Would you reveal your secret strategy to your competition, giving them all your intellectual property to use and then launch your idea before you do? You want to be a master and set the pace for others to follow or for you to be the go-to person. In the world

of commerce, as exemplified by tech competition between Apple and Samsung, secrecy and speed to market with an idea determines who has the larger market share. Do not be foolish by exciting yourself so much that you reveal confidential matters that can leave you defeated in your own game.

3. **Concentration of Force**

   a. **Military Strategy:** This strategy involves the concentration of combat power at decisive enemy locations and times that allow forces to achieve local superiority against the enemy, even if they are outnumbered. This principle is about applying overwhelming force to a critical enemy vulnerability.

   b. **Personal and Professional (Business) Application:** Know where to concentrate your efforts. When starting out on a purpose, a localised concentration at each progressive stage of the journey may enable you to achieve your purpose faster. On your roadmap discussed in Chapter Three, approach in progressive stages with the resources you have while maintaining your focus on the milestone for each stage.

4. **Economy of Force**

   a. **Military Strategy:** This strategy involves the efficient use of military resources, allocating them in a manner that achieves the desired outcome without waste. Resources, food, ammunition, medical supplies are distributed in a way that primary objectives receive the most focus and support, while secondary objectives are achieved with minimal necessary investment.

   b. **Personal and Professional (Business) Application:** Money, time, people, and raw materials are some of the resources you need to achieve your purpose. Using them resourcefully will ensure you have the liquidity that gives you the force you need to see your initiative to its finished state in the required time.

5. **Intelligence and Reconnaissance**

    a. **Military Strategy:** This strategy involves gathering and analysing information about the enemy's movements, strengths, weaknesses, and intentions. Through spy-tech, human spies and other covert means, intelligence is gathered. The aim is to make informed decisions and anticipate the enemy's actions in order to achieve conquest.

    b. **Personal and Professional (Business) Application:** Without data it is impossible to acquire the intelligence needed to perform any reconnaissance activity to achieve your purpose. Good and bad data provide information that could be invaluable to you. There is a reason why most organisations retain data for a long period of time, even after use, including good and bad data. When taking risks consciously, collect as much data as possible about the opportunity in relation to exploration and exploitation. Know the potential problems and issues you can encounter, and identify and understand the people you need by way of alliances you need to build. Use scenario analysis to anticipate the future possibilities and use that data to guide you in real terms.

6. **Psychological Operations**

    a. **Military Strategy:** This strategy aims to destabilise the morale, cohesion, and efficiency of enemy forces using things like propaganda, misinformation, and other psychological operations (psyops). Psyops were used by both Mongolians and Chinese to undermine enemy morale. The Mongols, for example, used fear as a weapon, spreading tales of their ferocity to terrify opponents. The Chinese used misinformation and deception, as outlined in Sun Tzu's *The Art of War*, to confuse and demoralise their enemies. The Ancient Assyrian empire, under some of the most sadistic kings, were ferocious warriors who used psyops to cripple their enemies with fear even before attacking them. According to historian W.B. Wright, 'Fighting was the business of the nation…' and psyops played a major part in it.

b. **Personal and Professional (Business) Application:** The best way to apply this is somewhat the opposite of the intended outcome of military psyops. In your case, you do not want to demoralise or confuse your audience, or maybe you do, depending on who and why. Ultimately, you want to understand the psychology of your audience or the people you engage with to a reasonable extent to allow you to serve them best and, in return, assist in achieving your purpose. This can inspire your audience to listen to you, respond positively to your message or buy from you when you use positive psychological cues that will engage them and lead them to the product or service that you are offering.

7. Build Alliances and Coalitions

a. **Military Strategy:** This strategy involves diplomatic efforts to secure allies, share intelligence, and coordinate military operations. It can significantly enhance the capability to project power and achieve common objectives quickly. The North Atlantic Treaty Organisation (NATO) is an example of how nations build alliances and coalitions to achieve a common purpose or mission together.

b. **Personal and Professional (Business) Application:** In a similar way, you want to build alliances and coalitions (relationships) with people who will work with you, assist you, inspire and motivate you to achieve your purpose. Knowing the 'who is who' in certain places of importance can open doors to key people of influence. Anyone who says they are self-made or that they single-handedly achieved success on their own is lying. I once saw a quote that read, 'Behind every successful woman is herself'. This is simply not true because every success requires people at all stages of the supply chain, including the buyer side. Appreciating the fact that we need people in varying capacities to achieve our purpose is a strength and essential skill required for success. These people are your 'purpose warriors', as I call them. Build them, appreciate them and go forth and conquer.

8. **Strategic Patience and Attrition**

   a. **Military Strategy:** You might have heard the term 'war of attrition', particularly in the news about the ongoing Russia–Ukraine war that began in February 2022. The aim of this strategy is to wear down the enemy over time through drawn-out, continuous pressure and military operations. This long-term approach relies on superior sustainability and endurance, hoping that the enemy will deplete their resources or wear them out to surrender.

   b. **Personal and Professional (Business) Application:** There are times you have to be willing to stay the course of a matter or be willing to play the long game to achieve your purpose, even when the odds seem to be stacked against you. Also, not all successes happen when we want them to happen. You have to understand the time dynamics for each purpose and work with them because external factors that you do not control play a key role in how and when things reach their stage of fulfilment. Build operational resilience, mental toughness, and emotional resilience, and maintain continuity of purpose until you have achieved a rewarding level of coverage of your risk territory map. This is fundamental to legacy building.

I have already shared a lot with you for creating an enriching life both on a personal and professional level. The onus is now on you to decide what to do with this information.

The Urgency of Now

'Echi eteka' is a saying in my native Igbo language that, directly translated, means 'Tomorrow is too far'. This phrase was used in reference to a deadly snake my uncle used to tell me about when I was a teenager living in Nigeria. It was likely a viper of some sort, whose bite is said to kill within minutes. The term 'echi eteka' is now commonly used in reference to anything that requires immediate action, not waiting for tomorrow, because the outcome of tomorrow could be fatal. That fatality could be the death of a person or a catastrophic failure of some sort due to delaying action or not responding appropriately to a situation or opportunity with the required urgency. Alongside that is another Igbo term, 'echi dị ime', which means 'Tomorrow is pregnant'. This phrase gives hope to the potential of tomorrow being pregnant with opportunities and rewards.

Using both 'echi eteka' and 'echi dị ime' in conjunction, you understand that you cannot wait for tomorrow to act on an opportunity because, by tomorrow, that opportunity or reward may no longer be present, leading to regret or, worse, great loss that could have a significant or catastrophic impact.

This idea of urgency in relation to opportunity, presented in this age-old Igbo philosophy, has fuelled the Igbo people to pursue opportunities in a way that no other tribe in Nigeria has, evident in their commercial prowess, thriving even in hostile regions. The Igbos, often referred to as the Jews of Africa, know how to take risks, just like ancient great merchants of old and modern-day merchants. Multi-billion and multi-trillion-dollar organisations today understand the 'urgency of now.' With this urgency in risk-taking approach, one needs to know the path to a favourable outcome. That outcome signifies the recognition that a person's or entity's current state needs to change to a desired state in the future. That desired state in the future is carved out on a mental or physical map of opportunities with multiple roadways and boundaries.

It is the first time I have mentioned boundaries in this book, and yes, it is important to note that there are boundaries one must recognise. This is not to say that these boundaries cannot or should not be breached, but to breach a boundary, you must know why, how, and what breaching a boundary would result in. Whether these are ethical boundaries, physical boundaries, mental boundaries, legislative boundaries, or regulatory boundaries, weighing the cost versus the rewards of breaching boundaries should be considered. I am in no way suggesting breaking the law here. There is a difference between breaking the law and breaching a boundary that must be understood.

Take, for example, these banks that are known to be globally reputable. BNP Paribas, Credit Suisse, Deutsche Bank, Goldman Sachs, and Wells Fargo all received fines in excess of US $3 billion for breaching regulatory boundaries, with BNP Paribas being the highest, fined US $8.9 billion for wilfully doing business with sanctioned countries. Did they knowingly breach this regulatory boundary? Yes. Did they take risks to act on the opportunity to do business with these countries? Yes. Did they act urgently? Yes. Did the reward of doing business with these countries outweigh the cost and fine received? Absolutely, yes! And you can consider this the sweet spot: No one went to jail or was put before a firing squad for breaching these boundaries.

According to United Nations data, about sixty-one million (61,000,000) people die every year. That is a daily average of about one hundred and sixty-seven thousand (167,000). It could be any one of us any day. 'Echi dị ime' with your opportunities and rewards, but you have to act now because 'echi eteka'.

CHAPTER FIVE

Inside the Risk Worlds

There are metaphysical questions about risk that no one else has answered or that most people do not care to ask or even seek answers to, such as: Why is there an economy even though we live in abundance? With so many opportunities for everyone to have an abundant life of riches, why are only a few people benefitting while the majority struggle to make ends meet? Why is there universal order and societal disorder? Why is the world so risky with too many problems? What are the worlds of risk? Who controls the world of risk? I have answered the biggest one of them in the opening chapters of this book, and that is, 'What is risk?' in Chapter One.

There are many worlds in the universe of risk that influence the way we live. Recognition of these worlds can be like the bright headlights of a car on a dark night that guide you and indicate your presence to other road users who may or may not have their headlights on. Our lives and the risks we take consciously and unconsciously cut across multiple landscapes or worlds.

Let us peer into some of the major worlds of risk in which we live and operate to get a better understanding of how they really work. This will help you take risks more effectively and achieve your purpose faster and with less friction.

The Health World

It is often said that health is wealth because it does not matter who you are or how much money you have. Whether you are a billionaire or not, one thing is certain: sickness and death. This is why the combined worth of the healthcare and pharmaceutical world or industry is worth trillions of dollars. The health of the population, good or bad, is big business. The health world is very complex, with both ethical and unethical complexities. A former doctor once told me that being a doctor was less about curing and more about treating symptoms and preserving life, even though cures exist. Contrary to popular opinion, it is not money that makes the world go round but health. If you have a sick population, the economy suffers losses, as was seen during the 2020 Coronavirus global outbreak. Health risk presents both opportunities and rewards on the upside, as well as major threats and problems on the downside.

Pharmaceutical companies, often referred to as 'Big Pharma', are central players in the health world, driving innovation in drug development, medical research, and healthcare delivery. While they contribute to medical breakthroughs and lifesaving treatments, they also face scrutiny over issues like drug pricing, marketing practices, and conflicts of interest. Balancing the pursuit of profit with ethical considerations remains a persistent challenge for Big Pharma.

Hospitals and clinics serve as frontline providers of healthcare services, delivering medical care, diagnostics, and treatments to individuals and communities. These institutions face challenges related to resource allocation, staffing shortages—often exacerbated by medical professionals embarking on industrial action due to low salaries—and financial sustainability, particularly in underserved regions. Despite these challenges, hospitals and clinics play a vital role in delivering essential healthcare services and responding to public health emergencies. Controversies arise occasionally when some medical professionals break away from conventional practice to offer cures through alternative methods and treatments.

Personally, I like to investigate my healthcare, ask questions, and do my own research before deciding on any treatment. In 2017, I had a back injury from lifting weights that caused me excruciating pain. During my visit to the doctor and after assessments were carried out, he suggested surgery and offered to prescribe codeine. I felt this was premature, given that the root cause of the pain had not been determined. I declined both the codeine and surgery and requested several scans. An x-ray and MRI were eventually carried out, which determined that I had an L5 S1 disc bulge in my spine. This was my first step to healing. Through shockwave treatment, musculoskeletal physiotherapy, and a conscious awareness of my health and well-being, I healed without surgery or any pain medication that could have had major side effects. If I had not been informed or sought information to make the appropriate decision on what treatment was correct for me, I might have been consigned to a lifetime of pain, medication, and mental health issues from making the wrong decision based on that doctor's recommendation.

A renowned pharmacist I know once told me that the 'entire medical practice and education is designed by and around the pharmaceutical industry'.

To take risks successfully, you have to be in the best health possible. Poor habits, such as popping painkillers at the onset of any pain, are a sign of weakness. Painkillers do not cure the real underlying problem; they simply mask it. The global pain-management drug market is estimated to be worth around $78 billion, rising to around $91 billion in 2029, with the citizens of the United States of America being the highest consumers. Turn on the TV, and every commercial is a drug-related advertisement for this pain or that. The same can be said about taking recreational drugs like cannabis, cocaine, or others to temporarily escape the realities of life. Risk-takers embrace the pain and work through it. Seek health through information to make the correct decision so you can stay on the path to achieving your purpose.

Pain is a signal; it is not the thing itself. Know what causes the pain and treat that if possible, and the pain will go away. This can be both literal and figurative.

Dan Clark, author of the book *The Art of Significance: Achieving the Level Beyond Success*, recovered from an American football training accident. He said, 'Pain is a signal to grow and not to suffer. When you learn the lesson pain teaches, the pain goes away. So, in life, there are no more mistakes but lessons.'

What I learned from this is that when you focus on pain or the consequences of bad health, you do not foster healing. There is a lesson here that involves learning about the 'pain' and the wisdom that comes from it, which can provide valuable healing benefits that are not only physical but, more powerfully, can be spiritual, emotional, mental, and psychological.

The Economy World

The economy is man-made, and most risk-taking is driven by local, national, and global economic systems. Underlying each economy are very powerful beneficiaries at the helm, much like a pyramid scheme. My assessment is that they influence how the world works and sometimes determine when to induce systemic shocks to steer the population of a nation or the world in a particular direction. When you study economic patterns carefully, you can elucidate or almost predict a systemic change happening and why it may be happening. Some of these changes happen stealthily, while others are more sudden, such as The Great Depression (1929–1939), Black Monday (1987), the 2008 Global Financial Crisis, and more recently, the COVID-19 Pandemic (2020 to 2022). Each of these events changed the usual way we operate. You just have to study patterns and always perform the 5W-Analysis: Why, What, Who, When, Where.

- Why is it happening?
- What is it meant to accomplish?

- Who is or are the drivers or beneficiaries?
- When will it start and end?
- Where will it happen or originate from?

Doing a deep analysis with these 5Ws will enable you to understand economic currents and equip you with information that will enhance your risk-taking abilities so that you can convert more opportunities you identify.

The Finance World

The finance world, although independent, is also integral to the functioning of the global economy, influencing everything from global economic growth to economic collapses and the impact it has on people and the development of societies and cultures. It is primarily about money in all its forms: the creation of money, the accumulation of it, the management and study of money, investments, and societal impacts.

When you think of the finance world, the first thing that comes to mind is the banks. Yes, the banks are a major part of this, but there are other financial entities at play in the finance world, such as wealth managers, family offices, investment managers, money transfer services, pension managers, peer-to-peer lending platforms, and the list goes on. The finance world carries a significant amount of both upside risk and downside risk. On the upside, there is the opportunity to make eye-watering amounts of money (more than many know what to do with). On the downside—which is what most people tend to focus on—is the potential for loss of money through frauds, scams, bad investment decisions and so on.

Here are three lessons I have learned from working with most of the main players in the finance world for over a decade now:

1. **Man makes money; money makes man mad.** When I heard this on a podcast from someone who had similarly worked in the finance world, I quickly recognised the industry of finance is the greatest

71

influencer of mankind and that if you can master it, you can move it, use it and live outside of it.

2. **The idea of being rich forever or generationally rich is deceptive for two reasons.** First, you will die one day and in death your money is worth nothing to you. Two, leaving huge sums of money to a generation deprives you of living and deprives them of earning.

3. **The finance world is a pyramid scheme.** Why does it exist? What is its purpose? Who are the controllers within? Where does it get its power and authority from? When will it collapse? Every pyramid scheme collapses one day.

The Geopolitical World

The geopolitical world is a risk landscape riddled with more downsides than upsides. With only a very small number of people in the upper and special class benefitting from the rewards of geopolitics, you may wonder what the benefits are. Geopolitics is traditionally the study of how political powers are reinforced or undermined by geographical arrangements such as boundaries, coalitions, spatial networks, and the exploitation of natural resources. The fact is that there are more threats and problems presented for the world's population than any projected value. Only a few profit from geopolitical tensions and conflicts. It is unethical to think that the killing of people and destruction of properties in conflict is a profitable business. With trillions of dollars pouring into this sector, government stakeholders, defence contractors, weapons manufacturers, resource exploiters, reconstruction firms, and infrastructure developers are destroyed. As a result, financial markets are some of the sources of profits from geopolitical conflicts.

When you examine, for example, the Russia–Ukraine conflict, you may be fooled into believing that this is just a territorial conflict. But when you lift up the hood, you uncover so much complexity that it is overwhelming to all parties involved. As time goes on, these conflicts almost become part of everyday living, which eventually gets made into a Hollywood movie or documentary, further profiting the beneficiaries of the movie and entertainment world.

As part of understanding 'how the world works', it is important to manage fear. Fear-mongering is a tool used to control and manipulate the populace. History repeats itself in many ways, and the same method of propaganda is still being used. The most powerful of them are the media houses used to induce fear. Fear has a price, and that price is paid to the originators of the fear when you give in to it. The fear of geopolitical conflicts can affect your ability to focus on your 'real purpose'. Your best response is to plan your reaction. Always ask yourself, *What if?* and put your prepared resilience plan in place if conflict erupts. Understand the current threats and the resulting problems if they occur. Identify the opportunities, which could include escape routes, sources of self-preservation in the event of a materialised conflict, survival kits, food, and money in cash. Maintaining neutrality while mastering how to use the data coming out of various sources can provide invaluable resources that can benefit you.

The Technology World

The technology world is a vast and ever-evolving landscape that encompasses a broad range of disciplines, including information technology (IT), artificial intelligence (AI), biotechnology, robotics, nanotechnology, and more, which influence risk-taking. It influences how we live, work, and interact with one another and our environment.

At its core, the technology world is fuelled by the relentless pursuit of knowledge and efficiency, aiming to solve complex problems, improve human life, and understand the universe more deeply. Innovations such as the internet, smartphones, and cloud computing have revolutionised communication, making it instantaneous and global. I remember the days of analogue phones and internet modems when you would need to fire up before you could get on the internet. Today, AI and machine learning are transforming industries by enabling smart automation, predictive analytics, and personalised experiences. In addition, advances in biotechnology and medical technology are paving the way for groundbreaking treatments and personalised medicine, hoping to extend life expectancy and improve the quality of life.

However, there are ethical concerns about how technology and medicine interact, such as genetic engineering, artificial wombs, human cloning, and neurotechnology and brain-computer interfaces (BCIs). Elon Musk is involved in neurotechnology and BCIs through his company Neuralink, which he co-founded in 2016. Neuralink's primary goal is to develop ultra-high bandwidth brain-machine interfaces to connect humans and computers, with a broader vision of facilitating symbiosis between human intelligence and artificial intelligence. Imagine inserting microchips into your brain or plugging your brain into a device through wires or wireless methods to make it function faster or operate at a higher level than humanly possible!

This rapid pace of technological advancements also brings significant threats and problems. In-person social interaction has plummeted, with most people hooked to their devices for virtually everything, including shopping, friendships, dating, reading, and doctor's appointments. Cybersecurity emerges as a critical concern, with the increasing prevalence of cyber-attacks exposing vulnerabilities in our digital infrastructure. Privacy issues are another significant concern, as the collection and analysis of vast amounts of personal data raise questions about consent and data protection, with concerns about whether the devices we use are spying on us. Moreover, the automation of jobs through AI and robotics poses potential threats to employment and economic stability, highlighting the need for societal adaptation and policy interventions.

Not every technology serves our purpose. As fascinating as they may be, it would be wise for you to evaluate your use of technology with the purpose you want to achieve.

The Religion World

Religion governs the lives of every human on earth today in one way or another. Religion is a complex and multifaceted ideology that generally comprises a set of beliefs, practices, and rituals related to the existence of one or more gods or supernatural entities. It often includes moral codes, cultural systems, and worldviews that shape and guide the behaviour and thinking of its followers.

The attitudes, beliefs, and practices of religion's followers may be personal, or they may be advocated by an organisation. Whether it is Catholicism, Islam, Protestantism, Anglicanism, Atheism, Agnosticism, Pentecostalism, Buddhism, Hinduism, Ancestorism, Jehovah's Witnesses, or any other, they have an effect on the things we do because the tenets of religion influence our moral compass, which in turn influences our risk-taking.

Some of the complexities that exist due to the array of many religious organisations include religious tensions, cultural sensitivities, and the impact of religious beliefs on social and political dynamics. Take, for example, the fighting for dominance between Catholics and Protestants, Islam and Christianity, Sunni Islam and Shia Islam, and Hindus and Sikhs. People and organisations operating in these diverse cultural contexts must navigate risks related to religious extremism, interfaith conflicts, and the intersection of religious values with business practices.

Consider the Israeli–Palestinian conflict, the effects of which ripple far across the globe. In 2021, I had the opportunity to work with some executives in Palestine from the banking and insurance sectors. During the course of delivering the training, I learned about the deep impact the religious conflict is having on the Palestinian economy, including the lack of a central bank, the complexity of having to use three currencies to trade, travel restrictions, and many more challenges.

For the foreseeable future, religious diversity will remain a part of life. Understanding this diversity and learning to navigate it to achieve your purpose will be essential to its impact on your life and organisation.

The Secret Society World

Secret societies are member-only organisations that operate under a certain level of secrecy, often requiring entry through special processes such as initiations. Secret societies have long been the subject of conspiracy theories. Members of secret societies often go on to occupy positions of power in the higher echelons of the world's stage. During my university years, secret societies, also referred to as fraternities, fought for dominance on campus, and those with superior power wielded more control over how things ran. Members who become successful in the corporate world or politics often favour fellow members by bringing them on board to create dominance in the outside world. Harvard, Yale, Cambridge, and Eton universities have these special clubs, fraternities, or secret societies, and members often look out for each other during and after their years at university.

Now, expand this to the wider world. There are political, criminal, and occult secret societies that play a significant role in the current world order in terms of how the world works. This is not to say that you have to join one to be successful. But it is a fact that if you want to access certain areas of society or enter into power at some levels, you may not achieve that if it is controlled by a secret society. As you take risks on the world stage, you need to understand how the world works, know who is who, what is what, and where is where to navigate better and achieve your purpose. The world is governed by very powerful forces. So, if you are holistically ethical, you would know that when things do not go in the direction you want, there may be an opposing force which may require you to think differently and act differently if you understand this. Consciously taking risks means that you are swimming in the opposite direction of the masses, and that means you will be easily noticed.

Your mental, emotional, physical and spiritual resilience needs to be fully operational.

I was fourteen when my father took me to his lodge. This was my first direct encounter with one of the world's significant secret societies. Living at home with a parent who gained access to the secret society world while in Portugal, I was able to observe the orderliness in how things were done. My father would try to instil that order in us, such as the 5 a.m. rise to start chores around the home and other things which I will not mention. What I noticed was that, at the time, my father's close colleagues and friends who belonged to the same lodge all favoured one another and had significant wealth. They held knowledge that allowed them to access parts of the world the rest of the population could not because they had been subjected to organised education through the schooling system. I have deliberately chosen not to mention the names of any groups. One way or another, secret societies have an impact on our lives and the risks we take.

The Media and Entertainment World

A fundamental resource for risk-taking is data. Data provides information or misinformation, and the media and entertainment world dish out information overtly and subliminally. The media and entertainment industries wield significant influence on the world's population, presenting both threats or problems and opportunities or rewards. What you need to pay attention to is the role this world plays in shaping public conversations, opinions, and behaviours. With the rise of digital media platforms and the proliferation of content consumption channels, you must address the challenges related to media bias, fake news, and the spread of disinformation presented through news media. If you pay attention and do a deep dive into mainstream media, you will find that most play a role in shifting political views or public opinions when it comes to major societal or world shifts, as is seen in political elections in most parts of the world. Due diligence with the information you receive is an intelligent thing to do before making decisions based on information gathered from the media.

It is dangerous to your mind to allow all forms of information to be absorbed. There is so much noise out there in the world right now that is readily available at our fingertips through our mobile devices. Social media is full of so much variety that you can find yourself surfing endlessly. My view is that if it does not serve you, it hurts you. Be intentional about the information you take in through whatever channels. Every bit of wasted time never comes back to you, so make it count.

The influence of media and entertainment is complex and multifaceted, deeply intertwined with societal structures and individual psychology. Its impact can be profoundly positive, offering avenues for learning, inspiration, and connection, but it also has the potential for negative effects on creativity and the achievement of one's purpose.

CHAPTER SIX

How to Suck the Breast of Kings, Queens and Nations to Get Really Good Milk

'And you will actually drink the milk of nations,
At the breast of kings you will nurse;
And you will certainly know that I, Jehovah, am your Saviour,
And the Powerful One of Jacob is your Repurchaser.
Instead of the copper I will bring in gold,
And instead of the iron I will bring in silver,
Instead of the wood, copper,
And instead of the stones, iron;
And I will appoint peace as your overseers
And righteousness as your task assigners.'
–Isaiah 60:16-17

This passage from the New World Translation of the Holy Scriptures holds the key to wealth as it should be: righteous wealth. When most people think about wealth, they attribute it mainly to material things, which is quite an ignorant way of perceiving or receiving wealth.

In this chapter, I will show you how and where you can access the 'milk' of opportunities and convert them to rewards.

For thousands of years, milk and honey have symbolised wealth, bringing with them a certain level of modesty and peace that gold and other precious materials, such as diamonds and platinum, do not. Those who explore and exploit milk rarely encounter the stresses or hazards faced by those who seek gold and other precious materials in very inhospitable and hazardous environments.

Without milk, most of mankind and other mammals would not exist today because it is the mother's milk that feeds them right after birth until they are weaned onto more solid food as maturity looms.

Breasts symbolise opportunity—an opportunity that lies in food and nourishment for a child. When hungry, the child knows just what to do. They hold their mother's breast with their hands, latch onto the nipple, and start to suck. Sometimes they suck so aggressively that they bite their mother's nipple, leaving it sore. This, by extension, symbolises our human attitudes towards the breast and the milk, represented as our home, the earth and the entire universe with what it has to offer us (the milk). The earth and the universe are ripe with the milk of opportunities, but what we have is an uneven equilibrium of the attraction and consumption of this wealth of milk. This has happened because the majority of the human population on earth have either relinquished their right to the opportunities that surround them because they do not know how to get them or are going for low-hanging fruits reachable by everyone else, which leads to scarcity very quickly. Therefore, they do not put in as much effort to reach farther or dig deeper to get the really good opportunities that give them their desired amount of wealth.

What this leads to is that those few who see this lack of foresight or inability to acquire wealth do the work and become extremely wealthy, thus having an unimaginable amount of wealth, while the rest of the population becomes spectators to these few who have, unbeknownst to them, taken something that could have been theirs. We can split the world's population into two kinds of babies: lazy suckers and aggressive suckers. The lazy suckers represent roughly about 80% of the human population, and the aggressive suckers are 20%. The lazy suckers are the majority of the population who do the bare minimum to get their share of 'milk' or opportunities and rewards, while the aggressive suckers are the very few who do not go for the low-hanging fruit where there is scarcity but instead leap to higher places of abundance where there is no scrambling for opportunities and rewards.

You may now start to question yourself. How do I move from a place of scarcity to a place of abundance? Let me show you how to do this in five simple steps, but before that, you need to be very clear on what the 'Breast' and 'Milk' represent and who these kings, queens, and nations are.

The 'Breast' of Opportunities

The breast represents the vast amounts of opportunities available on earth and in the wider universe to satisfy the needs and wants of every human being ever born from the beginning of time. You cannot get to the milk without first getting to the breast, and these 'breasts' of opportunities are on the kings, queens, and nations. This means that the order you follow to find the 'breast' of opportunities matters. First, you find kings, queens, and nations. Next, you have to find a way to seduce them in order for them to give you access to their breasts (the opportunities). Then, you do the work to get the milk out (the rewards).

What does this mean? It means that you need to seek out who or what (kings, queens, and nations) possesses the opportunities that will give you the return or rewards you seek. Then, you need to convince them to give you access to their entity or themselves. This could be their organisation, project, or a significant person of influence (the breast) for you to deliver your service, solution, or product. In return, you get the rewards or payment (the milk) for the work you have done. The output you get determines the kind of sucker you are: lazy sucker or aggressive sucker.

The 'Milk' of Rewards

Milk simply represents, as I have alluded to above, the payment, rewards, or return you get for the work you have performed, the amount of opportunities you have converted to rewards. This could be as simple as the amount of money made from the products and services you sell, to the power you gain to influence people on a larger scale, global recognition and prestige, or access to exclusive resources that are not open to anyone else.

The Kings, Queens, and Nations

Kings, queens, and nations represent the people and places that hold access to the opportunities (breasts) that will give you the rewards (milk) you seek. The profile of these kings, queens, and nations varies. They include company owners, CEOs, executives of companies, government officials such as politicians, right down to your next-door neighbour. Whoever holds the key to the opportunities you seek is the king or queen. But nations? Nation here represents a location. You may be more of an exploratory risk-taker, meaning that what you seek may be buried under the ground somewhere or on land, such as gold diggers and farmers. In this case, you may not need a king or queen to seduce; you are your own king and queen who has the opportunity to create rewards using the resources you have. But you may need a licence or permission before you can exploit a land for its resources. If so, you need to seduce the king or queen of that land.

Let us now consider five powerful ways to get your 'milk'.

Step One: Before the Milk

To be able to get milk, you need to understand the process of fertility. In a biological sense, if you are a man, you need to find a fertile female to mate with. If you are a woman, the same rule applies. Similarly, you need to find the potential fertile king, queen, or nation who holds the opportunities that will get you the rewards you want. To do this, you must have a clearly defined purpose that you are en route to achieving by following your roadmap. The kings, queens, and nations must be aligned with your purpose, meaning they hold the resources and/or opportunities that will enable you to achieve your purpose.

Prior to becoming clear on what my purpose and vision were, I pursued kings, queens, and nations that were not in alignment with what I was creating. I was simply focusing on the monetary aspect of what I would get from them and was not offering real value, which led to some serious lessons learned, thankfully. Upon defining my purpose (to unveil and empower people with risk so they can achieve their purpose) supported by a laser-clear vision (to become the world's most trusted risk influencer), the pathway to getting consistent milk became clear and unobstructed by anything or anyone but me, and the foundation was well set just as dried cement. Once you have found the kings, queens, and nations, you need to seduce them.

Step Two: The Opportunity. The Seduction. The Mammary of Life.

You have identified the person, people, or place that holds the key to the opportunities you want. What next? Seduction! Seduction is a vital aspect of everyday life. Most of humanity is the result of some form of seduction. Getting this wrong could mean a total loss of opportunities, which could critically impact the potential of your purpose being achieved. Be aware that every king or queen is curious or cautious, so this is where you put your power of seduction to use. Seduction does not mean deception. It is the process you go through to build a relationship with your potential 'Purpose Mate' (the king or queen aligned with your purpose). You have to get them to see that you are the right partner for them by demonstrating mutual interest, the value you will bring to them, and why you are the best mate for them in relation to your purpose and theirs. Ultimately, their submission to you gives you access to their breast, enabling you to maintain seduction until you get the milk that fulfils your purpose.

Step Three: Put Your Mouth Where the Milk Is— Exploring Opportunities

Aiming for the right opportunities requires a bit of due diligence on your part. You need to understand the anatomy of opportunities by recognising the actual opportunities in a person, people, or place. I call this the value-for-profit mentality. What does that mean? It means that your mindset has to be set on making a profit or getting a reward for every opportunity you find. Sometimes, you find opportunities through active engagement; other times, opportunities come to you through encounters with a king, queen, or nation. That means being switched on *all the time.* Wherever you go—whether on holiday, on a plane, or in the supermarket—you have to be switched on and always ready to put your mouth where the milk is.

Putting your mouth where the milk is means not just grabbing hold of the breast but aiming the nipple to your mouth in preparation to get that good milk out. How? You must know what to say to seduce the king or queen in question, know when to speak and respond to an opportunity, and when to allow the other person to speak to give you data through what they say. This enables you to qualify the opportunity for its value. You also need to recognise the time factor in the opportunity process. Every opportunity is time-bound, and you must know when the opportunity life cycle begins and be on cue to enter it at its time with the catalytic elements that will produce the outcome you want. This happened to me a few years ago when I was approached by a former client's husband, who was a government security consultant in Malaysia. She had spoken to her husband about me following the completion of our project because they were pleased with the results I delivered. He presented me with the opportunity to work with the largest advertising mogul in Malaysia. At that time, this opportunity seemed so big that I felt it was above me due to its multinational and cross-border legal complications. I thought to myself: *I am not ready for a project of this magnitude because I do not feel equipped to give this potential client the value they seek.* Being ethical is the best thing to do in situations like that to maintain integrity and trust. When you find yourself in a situation where you feel you are not ready for an opportunity because it might seem too big, just step back for a minute and think about it. Consider the possibility of working with someone who could boost your capability by way of a partnership, as long as the opportunity can be exploited ethically. Failing to act on cue with the correct corresponding action is the reason why many fail to achieve their purpose or, at best, remain at a mediocre level. These opportunity dynamics are essential for risk-taking.

Step Four: Suck It Well—Exploiting Opportunities

This step indicates that your seduction has paid off because you have metaphorically been allowed access to take hold of the king or queen's breast full of opportunity. It is now time to put your mouth on and figuratively suck it to get the milk out. Just like babies have to put in the work to suck out the milk from their mother's breast to be fed, you have to now do the work to convert the opportunities that you have been given access to into the benefits and rewards it offers both you and the person or people involved. Managing your stakeholders' interests is essential for you to continue to have access to draw out the figurative milk, which is typically measured in financial terms. Exploitation follows exploration. Exploitation begins when you commence the operation to turn the opportunity into the desired outcome, typically measured in the amount of revenue or profits made from the sale of a product or service.

Step Five: Let the Milk Flow—Count Your Blessings

Accounting for the amount of rewards is more than the balance sheet. Keeping the tap of rewards flowing is an art that is both satisfying and essential to the maintenance and growth of your purpose. There are five things you need to do to keep the milk flowing. They are:

1. **Count Your Blessings**: Account for every return and reward achieved. Know how much came in, and measure it in comparison with any benchmarks set.

2. **Apportion Your Rewards**: Allocate some of the rewards from the opportunity to the king and queen who allowed you to seduce them with your proposition. Allocate some for yourself and other beneficiaries to maintain the loyalty of your 'purpose mates'—those who are aligned with your purpose and helped bring it to fruition.

3. **Reinvest the Rewards**: A significant amount of the rewards you make should be reinvested back into the entity or the vehicle being used to deliver the purpose. This may be the company you are using.

4. **Succession Planning**: Knowing when to step aside, not step out, is transitioning from one purpose to another, using the purpose you have achieved as a latch to link up to a greater purpose—continued access to the king, queen, or nation, or access to more powerful kings, queens, or nations. At this point, you become a master of the purpose you have achieved and need to move up and forward beyond that purpose to avoid devaluing what you have already achieved. A great example of this is Bill Gates, the former CEO of Microsoft. He outgrew Microsoft and used it as a stepping stone for greater purposes, such as the Bill & Melinda Gates Foundation, among other significant purposes in which he is currently very active. Knowing when you have outgrown an already achieved purpose is fundamental to how you further evolve as a person or an entity.

5. **Dynamic Risk-Taking:** To keep the milk of rewards flowing, optimise your seductive powers to access further 'breasts' of opportunities to release their rewards. This level of risk-taking demonstrates that you possess elite-level wisdom available to only a few and have taken risks that very few take through self-discipline to achieve a level beyond success. This is master seducer status, where you dine with kings and queens and have at your control the wealth of nations.

CHAPTER SEVEN

Learn Lessons from Crop Growers and Their Seven Steps for Bountiful Rewards

For everything that exists, there is a defined law that operates it, or that has to be followed to achieve a defined outcome. We sometimes refer to these as 'processes' we ought to follow. Laws of nature have been mirrored or copied, leading to some of the greatest inventions by humans. The study of aerodynamics in birds led innovators to create aeroplanes and further enhance aviation. The shape of the kingfisher's beak, which allows it to dive into water with minimal splash, inspired the design of the nose on Japan's Shinkansen bullet trains. The echolocation abilities of bats have influenced the development of sonar and radar technologies. By studying how bats navigate and hunt using sound waves, scientists were able to develop systems that use sound to detect objects underwater or in the air, which is particularly useful in navigation for ships and submarines. These are just a few examples of natural laws and designs that have been copied by scientists and have inspired various innovations and technological advancements. These advancements have brought many rewards to humans, such as improvements in transportation, safety, economic growth, and more.

What can you and I, everyday humans, copy or follow to achieve our purpose? Most people turn to education, going as far as university degrees, but end up empty or not knowing what to do next. Unfortunately, hundreds of millions of people who have graduated from university end up in jobs that are unrelated to their field of study or working in non-graduate jobs. The Chartered Institute of Personnel and Development (CIPD) reported that about 58.8% of UK graduates are in jobs deemed to be non-graduate roles. Now, expand that to a worldwide audience, and what you get is trillions of dollars wasted on university education that did not yield the intended benefit.

Let us solve that problem by once again mirroring or copying a simple process that has been in existence, tried and tested, and always yields results: farming! Farmers are material risk-takers because, without them, the impact on humanity would be catastrophic. Their purpose, to provide food for humanity, is a clear one. I remember as a young teenage boy in Port Harcourt, Nigeria, when my mother would take us to farm crops on huge acres of land and rear chickens and turkeys. There was always an input and an output. You plant, you reap more than you planted. You invest, you get a return.

Start with a clearly defined purpose, and then take the following seven steps that you can apply in your life or in a professional capacity.

Step One: Identify Your Seeds

You have probably heard the term 'seed money'. This metaphor from farming means the money that is given to someone to help them start a new business or project. Just as a discerning farmer selects the appropriate seeds that will prosper in the upcoming season, you must meticulously choose your 'seeds'—that is, your purpose, the ideas, goals, missions, or projects you desire to cultivate. This pivotal step determines the outcome you receive as a reward when it matures. Your 'seeds' must align with your purpose and the tools or expertise you possess, preparing you for the journey that lies ahead and the harvest you reap.

Step Two: Select The Right Land for Your Seeds

For a farmer to succeed, they must understand that some plants require different soil types, temperatures, topography, and so on for that seed to do well. The same applies to you. Identifying the optimal environment for your 'seeds' to flourish goes beyond mere physical locations. It is about pinpointing where your ideas, abilities, and ambitions can find an appreciative audience and the conditions to thrive. This milieu might be a specific community, workplace, or niche market. Understanding the terrain, its requirements, obstacles, and prospects is similar to a farmer's understanding of the soil. It is about determining where your contributions can take root and prosper, ensuring a positive impact and achieving sustainable growth.

Step Three: Use the Right Technique for Your Seeds

There is an abundance of processes, methods, frameworks, and models that claim to have the best approach for you to accomplish your purpose. One thing I have learned is that no one knows my purpose or what I want to achieve better than I do, just as a farmer knows what seed he wants to plant and what he expects to get from it. Identifying and using the correct technique or approach for nurturing your seed ideas, goals, and mission is as critical as the seeds you sow. It requires the mastery of techniques that will bring your goals to fruition. This could involve drawing up a carefully crafted roadmap, following it through, adapting it to external stresses that may occur, continuous learning, collaborations with other experts, and much more. By refining and using the right techniques, you are enriching your soil of opportunity, making it ready to give you the rewards of your initiatives.

Step Four: Take the Risk and Plant Your Seed

Take the risk and do the work. Planting your 'seeds' signifies a moment of bravery and commitment to take risks. It epitomises the point when you step forth to transform your plans into action. Like a farmer who plants in tune with the seasons, it is crucial to discern the appropriate timing for your risk-taking, that is, your action. At this point, you have commenced activities, putting yourself and your resources to work by performing the activities in the first phase of your journey on your roadmap. The farmer does not procrastinate because they know they have to act in relation to the seasons. A farmer would not plant in autumn a crop meant to be planted in spring. When it was farming season in Nigeria, we would wake up very early in the morning to go farming, planting main crops like cassava, corn, and yams, either digging the ground with manual instruments like hoes or making ridges, depending on what was being planted. We took the risk, did the work all day, and harvested. This early introduction to farming led me to identify further opportunities that created income for me at an early age. Time was of the essence. Do not mess around with procrastination because the seasons of success will not wait for you.

Step Five: Nurture Your Seed Investment

At this stage, you should be actively fostering the growth of your ventures. Your seed investment requires continued commitment, time, and effort to ensure it continues to grow or, in your case, continues to progress on your roadmap towards achieving your purpose. Every farmer nurtures their 'seed'. They feed it. Besides the natural laws playing their part, they do things like use manure, eliminate pests, and encourage pollination. Whether it is plants, poultry, cattle, or anything else, they have to nurture it. You have to recognise the natural laws of risk-taking in the pursuit of your purpose and supplement them by taking the necessary nurturing actions to maintain the trajectory towards the success you seek. Nurturing your 'seeds' demands attentiveness and adaptability to provide the budding shoots of your labour with everything they require to flourish. Your 'seed' has a life of its own, and you need to create synergy with it even though you are the initiator of its growth.

Step Six: Protect Your Seed Investment

Most farmers have some type of protection around their produce. Some farmers have dogs patrolling their farmlands to protect livestock. You need to do the same thing. As a farmer safeguards their produce or livestock during its growth stage, you must protect your ideas, projects, and ultimate purpose by implementing defences against potential threats, be they competitive pressures, changing trends, people who would steal your assets (whether intellectual or physical), or personal adversities. It is about remaining vigilant and proactive in maintaining the integrity and potential of what will give you the success you need to achieve your purpose.

Step Seven: Harvest at the Right Time—Reaping What You Sow

In 2015, I took a six-month sommelier course with the UK Sommelier Association. During this course and several vineyard and winemaker explorations, one of the vital lessons I learned was that in viticulture, harvesting grapes at the right time is crucial because it significantly influences the quality and flavour of the wine. Sugar content, acidity, phenols, flavour development, and wine styles all depend on the timing of the grape harvest. If not picked in time, all the 'blood, sweat, and tears' put into having a successful harvest could be wasted, having a catastrophic impact on the winemaker. Many winemakers have experienced significant losses due to late harvests. At this stage in your progress towards achieving your purpose, your seed would have matured into a final offer for the intended audience. Whether it is a product or service, timing its entry into the market is crucial because consumer behaviour is a psychology influenced by many factors and could impact your ability to generate the volume of sales you require to achieve your purpose.

Bonus Step: The Pigeon Sugar Water Effect

This is the simple science of keeping your audience coming back to you for more of what you are offering them, they also include the kings and queens mentioned earlier.

While working on my family's poultry farming business during my teenage years, I identified an unusual opportunity that not only fuelled my desire for entrepreneurship—though I did not know what the word 'entrepreneurship' meant then—but also taught me a valuable lesson, which I will share after telling the story. I learned about pigeon farming and started my own pigeon farm. I sourced a few male and female pigeons, and with the short hatch time for their eggs, about 20 days, I had many pigeons to sell in no time. This was a low-cost opportunity for me because I did not have to spend anything on feeding them; I just let them eat the chicken food from the poultry. However, there was one vital thing I did: I gave the pigeons water spiked with sugar, which they loved. This meant that they always came back whenever they flew out in the daytime, and on several occasions, they even brought back new friends, increasing my stock.

The lesson? It is not enough to take your offer to your audience or just to sell what your offer is. You have to take them to the next level of excitement that stimulates a part of their brain not excited by other offerings that come to them, making them always think about you and return to you when they need that fix. Pigeons do not need sugar water to survive; they would do just fine with regular water, which they can get anywhere. The sugar water was my unique selling point to the pigeons, and they kept coming back for more, even bringing a few friends along. Be unique in your offer and give 'sugar water' to your audience, and they will keep coming back to you, even bringing a few friends along.

CHAPTER EIGHT

How to Maintain Resilience and Continue to Take Risks When Crises Happen

Crises, whatever they may be, can be a soul-crushing experience for a person or an organisation, especially when they are not planned for. There are crises that we bring upon ourselves based on the decisions we make, crises that other people cause us, and crises that are outside our control. Regardless of the crisis dynamics, we can prepare for them, recover from them, find opportunities in them, and grow from them. For example, when the global health crisis caused by the coronavirus outbreak happened, most of us were not ready. This crisis stress-tested the resilience of people and organisations around the entire world physically, emotionally, mentally, infrastructurally, and in many other ways.

How do we maintain resilience? The most important thing to note is that resilience does not start when a crisis happens; it starts before a crisis. Anticipating crises of any sort is an essential part of risk-taking. It demonstrates your astuteness in protecting your purpose from being effaced by a crisis. You may wonder, *Does that mean I have to think about negative things or bad things that could happen to me?* Yes! Thinking is productive; worrying is counterproductive. I think about potential crises all the time so that I am ten steps ahead of them, or at least not shocked out of my systems if they were to happen. I would have already thought about them and psychologically developed some resilience to them without implementing any formal controls. This is a primary activity that we all need to embrace and perform both consciously and unconsciously. Let us look at resilience from several standpoints.

Seven for Perfection - Purpose Resilience

In 1919, Charles Leiper Grigg was employed by Vess Jones' manufacturing company. It was there that Grigg created and launched his first soft drink, an orange-flavoured concoction for a Vess Jones-owned company, Whistle.

Charles Leiper Grigg resigned from his position (passing up Whistle) following a disagreement with management and began working as a flavouring agent developer for soft drinks at the Warner Jenkinson Company. Next, Grigg created Howdy, his second soft drink. He brought his soft drink, Howdy, with him when he finally left Warner Jenkinson Co.

Grigg then went on to start the Howdy Company with banker Edmund G. Ridgway. Grigg had thus far created two soft drinks with an orange flavour. However, his carbonated beverages faced competition from Orange Crush, the reigning orange pop beverage. When Orange Crush expanded to control the orange soda market, Grigg was unable to compete.

Then he took a risk and finally made the decision to concentrate on lemon-lime flavours, a different, risky, and new product in the Orange Crush-dominated beverage market. Grigg created a brand-new beverage known as 'Bib-Label Lithiated Lemon-Lime Sodas' by October 1929. The moniker '7 UP Lithiated Lemon Soda' was swiftly adopted, and in 1936, it was altered once more to just '7 UP', which proved to be an absolute greatest-of-all-time drink.

7 UP is one of the most popular brands of drinks available today following Coca-Cola. Imagine what would have happened if Grigg had given up. We would not know what 7 UP is today.

The crises that he encountered during the process of trying to establish or achieve a purpose did not stop him from trying. He maintained resilience towards achieving the purpose of having a successful soft drink that would become a global household name. That is what risk-takers do. We must have the mindset to recover. It is important to know that an attempt at a particular goal, mission, or purpose can be adapted or changed if it becomes necessary.

Refine and Strengthen Your Purpose - Risk Resilience

In the midst of a crisis, it is important to revisit and critically evaluate your core purpose. This requires a meticulous appraisal of all elements that contribute to the realisation of the purpose, such as your vi, the strategic roadmap, objectives, and mission. These may require recalibration due to a materialised crisis, necessitating fresh perspectives and lessons learned. Here are some ways to refine and strengthen your purpose:

- **Conduct a Thorough Review:** Engage in a detailed assessment of your current purpose and goals. This should involve scrutinising your existing strategies, resources, and outcomes to determine how they align with the core values and objectives of your organisation.

- **Get Some Feedback:** Gather insights from a broad range of stakeholders, including employees, customers, and partners. Their perspectives can provide valuable feedback on what aspects of your purpose resonate well and what areas might need recalibration.

- **Identify the Lessons Learned:** Analyse the recent crisis to extract key lessons and insights. Determine what opportunities were revealed and what threats (weaknesses) were exposed. Use this analysis to refine your purpose to better meet the challenges of both the present and future.

- **Align with Core Values:** Ensure that your refined purpose is closely aligned with the fundamental values of the risks you are taking. Whether it is recognition, profits, integrity, loyalty, trust, or sustainability, this alignment enhances authenticity and consistency, which are crucial for building trust and engagement with the audience to your purpose and how it aligns with theirs.

- **Go for Goals:** Once your purpose has been refined, create the goals as mentioned in Chapter Three of this book. This helps to provide you with a clear direction and bite-sized or meaty milestones that motivate you and your purpose warriors to increase and maintain their risk-taking appetite during the journey to your purpose, no matter what happens along the way.

No Auto-Pilot - Operational Resilience

Your roadmap is the trusted guide or map you need that contains targets, goals, and milestones to reach your destination, that is, your purpose. Your roadmap is like your satellite navigation tool for getting to your purpose, and you have to be ready for obstacles along the way. To create your roadmap, you need to know your goals and milestones, and then you need to work out the timeline by which each target, goal, and milestone needs to be achieved. Your goals are homeless if they are not contained in a roadmap that is aligned with a purpose.

At the end of the day, your purpose delivers a mission: to serve. This means providing a service or product to a group of people. Having this service mindset or mentality, knowing that you are satisfying the needs of customers and clients, gives you a meaningful purpose. Create your roadmap to be resilient by anticipating the possibilities on the journey to your purpose. It is important to understand that your roadmap is the navigation to achieving your purpose, which is travelled by many. Your roadmap is not static, so you must design it to pick up opportunities along the way, anticipate threats, and plan your responses to them to avoid problems that could snap your purpose away from you. You may have to make deviations when a crisis happens, but it should not alter your focus from the purpose.

It is similar to when you drive your car or motorbike on a road trip and encounter a roadblock. Your most likely action is to take a diversion off your intended route and choose a different one while still maintaining focus on your purpose. This demonstrates your resilience in how you operate to achieve your purpose using the resources at your disposal: the people (you and your purpose warriors), the process (your roadmap), the systems (associated technologies), and any external factors outside your control that you must be aware of.

Whatever vehicle, channel, or entity you are using to achieve your purpose, whether it is a company you work for or a business you manage or own, the soundness of it is essential for the journey towards achieving the defined purpose.

Use Crisis To Strengthen Your Resilience

Crisis strengthens resilience. When you go to the gym to work out, that is putting a crisis on yourself in a sense because you're putting stress on yourself to gain better health. It is the same in life. A crisis will create certain stresses. It will create stress on your mind, body, business, work, home, or whatever it is. If you think about it, every top CEO you can name goes through some type of stress. However, to be able to operate on the world stage, your resilience is tested in many ways.

Think about Jeff Bezos and his running of a multimillion-dollar global company while dealing with personal challenges unrelated to business. That does not stop him from running Amazon and everything related. Having mental toughness is part of what risk-takers need to get through a crisis. Elon Musk deals with the emotional challenges of child custody and an estranged daughter but still performs optimally, runs his multibillion-dollar companies, thinks critically, and creates successes to be in the top three of the world's richest people in 2024, as recorded by *Forbes* magazine. See crises as an opportunity to strengthen your resilience; it could unlock the potential that requires just that level of stress.

Use Stress Testing and Scenario Analysis Before Crisis

Stress testing is a term used in risk management to indicate that a product or service has undergone rigorous testing. For example, let us consider your mobile phone. It would have undergone a drop test, a scratch test, and a waterproof test, among others. Stress testing involves subjecting a product or service to various stresses to determine its resilience and ability to meet consumer demands.

Scenario analysis is used alongside stress testing or independently. It is a continuous assessment of potential events that could positively or negatively impact your purpose. It involves asking 'what if' questions, such as 'What if it rains?' or 'What if my car breaks down?' It is not just about identifying potential issues but also planning responses. For example, 'What if I go to pitch to this client and the client does not turn up? Then what do I do?' It is crucial to regularly carry out scenario analyses, especially for business owners.

Crises can reveal weaknesses in your life, business, organisation, or purpose. Use these revelations as an opportunity to rebuild and improve. Proactively use ongoing crises as stress tests to build resilience. Understand your weaknesses and avoid useless shortcuts. Consider the audience you are serving and the potential for future crises. Your goal should be to ensure your product or service can withstand the tests of time and crises. When a crisis negatively impacts your product or service, use it as an opportunity to build it back better.

CHAPTER NINE

How to See More When Others See Less

The practice of measuring risk is not widely known or used by many today, except by mathematicians, statisticians, or analysts. Many so-called risk managers are clueless about how to measure risk and often default to using ranges in a risk matrix that typically provides an incorrect value of risk based on the negative impact it could have if it were to happen.

Know Your Risk Under Management

With many years of experience working with organisations, particularly in banking and finance, the term 'Assets Under Management' (AUM) is commonly used in relation to the investment of assets. This term refers to the market value of financial assets or investments that a wealth manager or financial organisation manages for its clients. Clients pay the entity managing their investments a fee for as long as those financial assets or investments are being managed. This indicates that to have assets under management, you need to be making or have some type of investment in a financial institution.

Risk Under Management (RUM) is different because everyone has access to it.

So, what is Risk Under Management? It is the total value of risk exploitation you are taking to achieve your purpose. This is a new concept adapted from the term 'assets under management'. AUM, as defined above, is a component of Risk Under Management. Your Risk Under Management includes all the qualified and quantified opportunities that you have and will use to realise, maintain, and expand your purpose. Your Risk Under Management includes liquid and hard assets, intellectual properties, talents, skills, natural gifts, and anything else that you have and can offer to a person or group of people to satisfy their needs or wants, giving you a return for that offer, typically in the form of money, other legal tender like cryptocurrency, or other rewards. Risk Under Management extends beyond the remit covered by assets under management and provides everyone with an opportunity to assess and quantify their worth in weight.

Knowing your Risk Under Management begins with undertaking a comprehensive assessment of the risks you are taking to achieve your purpose. Unlike traditional risk management, which primarily aims to mitigate only negative outcomes, Risk Under Management emphasises the exploitation of your risk opportunities that can generate increased value. Recognising these opportunities as components of RUM helps in understanding their potential to be weighted just as you would with precious metal or stone. Companies such as banks do a great job of knowing and quantifying everything that brings in revenue and profits. Individuals only need to mirror this by identifying those assets within themselves that are incomes-not-yet-earned but are awaiting the action that needs to be taken to acquire the income from the opportunities once the correct action is taken.

Price the Assets in Your Risk Under Management

My youngest daughter has creative skills in making jewellery, but when she prices her pieces, she often sets a very low price because she wants to make selling them easier, making the effort put into creating them higher than the reward, resulting in a loss. When I taught her the value of effort, time, and raw materials, she understood and adjusted her prices accordingly.

Pricing the assets in your Risk Under Management is about measuring the return on your investment from all the opportunities you identified and converted into measurable benefits. Quantifying them enables you to know your total revenue and profits gained. It helps measure the sustainability of your brand, whether personal or organisational.

Pricing the assets within your Risk Under Management involves assigning value to the opportunities you have identified. This process transforms something abstract into tangible and intangible assets that can be managed strategically to create wealth.

For example, what is the ability to speak multiple languages worth? Let us assume your native language is English, and in addition, you were taught to speak Mandarin, Russian, and Arabic, becoming fluent in all four languages by age ten. This multilingual ability is an asset you can capitalise on, opening you up to opportunities such as cross-cultural consulting, starting a language school (whether online or in-person), running a travel or tourism agency, working for international government agencies, and more. By taking the correct actions on any of these opportunities, you can convert them into rewards that pay you and, most importantly, set you apart from the masses competing for the same opportunities as you.

Let us demonstrate risk under management mathematically with a simple formula to show you how to calculate its value.

$$RUM = (OI \times EV) - C$$

Explanation:
- RUM: Risk Under Management.
- OI: Total number of opportunities identified.
- EV: Estimated value of each opportunity.
- C: Total cost associated with converting and managing the opportunities.

Example:

Suppose you have identified 10 opportunities of varying kinds (OI = 10), with an estimated value of £10,000 each (EV = £10,000). The total cost associated with these opportunities is £20,000 (C = £20,000).

1. Calculate the total value of identified opportunities:
   Total Value = OI x EV = 10 x 10,000 = £100,000

2. Subtract the total costs to explore the opportunities in your RUM:
   RUM = Total Value - C = 100,000 - 20,000 = £80,000

Therefore, your Risk Under Management (RUM) is £80,000.

Knowing the value of your Risk(s) Under Management is essential for making important decisions about the activities you perform to derive the rewards therein, as you will find in the Risk Funnel diagram in the next section.

The Risk Funnel

The concept of funnels has long been used in business to describe activities related to generating potential buyers, known as lead generation. In the process of risk-taking, attracting and engaging with the audience, you need to reach your purpose and maintain it, which partly depends on consistently satisfying the end-user's needs and wants. Sales funnels attempt to give people and businesses a way of doing this but have failed and misled hundreds of millions of people worldwide, seeking to capitalise on opportunities that will generate rewards for them.

A sales funnel, as it is commonly known, is a marketing concept that describes the journey potential customers go through on their way to purchasing a product or service, and does not incorporate the purpose of the risk-taker and the roadmap they follow to achieve their purpose.

A common flaw of the sales funnel is that it gets users to depend on others for their success. Users of sales funnels rely on tools or processes built by so-called marketing and sales gurus, forcing them to take a path that diverts them away from their purpose, leaving many frustrated after spending so much time and money to generate leads. One thing about the lead generation process that irks me is that marketers promise you qualified leads but are unable to support you through to conversion. Metrics of conversion are also deceptive and do not translate into actual rewards. For example, a meeting or a phone call with a potential client is classified as a converted opportunity even though it does not put a single dime in your pocket. I find this to be really deceptive.

The risk funnel is different! It is based on what you have and what you can control, and anyone can use it.

A risk funnel is a system that represents the production processes your opportunities must go through to become rewards, considering key factors such as Force, Time, and Flow. Where 'Force' is the effort used to process opportunities (including human resources, financial resources, technology resources, etc.), 'Time' is the period it takes to take an opportunity from its identified state to its real converted state, measured in the rewards it gives; and 'Flow' is the rate of converted opportunities produced in a given time. I use flow to describe opportunity in a liquid state before it becomes a reward in a state that brings the desired value. Flow rate, therefore, can be further described as the amount of processed opportunity over a given time.

This system was illustrated by Jesus Christ and recorded over 2000 years ago in the Gospel book of Matthew 7, Verses 13 and 14, where it describes a funnel-like approach for the attainment of the good life: 'Go in through the narrow gate, because broad is the gate and spacious is the road leading off into destruction, and many are going in through it; whereas narrow is the gate and cramped the road leading off into life, and few are finding it.'

Note that there are two channels spoken about by Jesus: a broad road, which can be likened to the wide compartment of the funnel, and a narrow road, which can be likened to the narrow part of a funnel. What is significant in this Bible verse are two kinds of activities or responses people take to getting the reward of life: *'leading off'* and *'finding it'*. You are being led off by 'forces', away from life to destruction, or you actively do something to find and gain 'life'. As you can see, some sort of processing is required to move from one state to another. That processing is the result of *Force, Time,* and *Flow*.

The practicality and operation of The Risk Funnel are supported by the laws of physics. In a typical funnel, gravity is the primary *force* that causes substances to move from the wide mouth down through the narrow spout. The *flow* rate is influenced by gravity, pressure differences, and the viscosity of the substance, while *time* describes the duration of the flow process.

Similarly, with a risk funnel, natural forces such as time, opportunity characteristics, environmental forces, operational forces, and psychological forces play a significant role in processing opportunities through the funnel to produce the rewards within them. All these forces are combined and summed up dynamically in the action you take to turn the opportunity into the reward that pays you over the time it takes to be fully processed.

Time is a form of force that should never be underestimated in risk-taking.

There are four key components in The Risk Funnel:

1. **Wide Mouth (Opportunity Vessel):** This is the initial stage of The Risk Funnel, holding your Risk Under Management, represented by all the opportunities you have, whether identified or unidentified, regardless of their source or certainty.

2. **Force, Time, and Flow (Action Taken and Action Dynamics):** This element signifies the combined deliberate and strategic actions applied to the opportunities in order to convert them to rewards. These include but are not limited to, threat mitigation, problem management, stress testing, scenario analysis, resource management,

work effort, strategies, and processes utilised to capitalise on and convert these opportunities into rewards.

3. **Narrow Spout (Reward Outlet):** This part of The Risk Funnel demonstrates the result of *Force, Time,* and *Flow,* showing opportunities that have been processed for the production of rewards.

4. **Reward Outlet (Future State, Realised Benefits and Purpose Achievement):** The final part of The Risk Funnel represents the successful conversion of opportunities into quantifiable rewards. Now you 'can hold it in your hand'. What you worked so hard for has started to yield actual quantifiable rewards. You no longer have opportunities at this stage but rewards. This is the beginning of the achievement of your purpose. See diagram of The Risk Funnel.

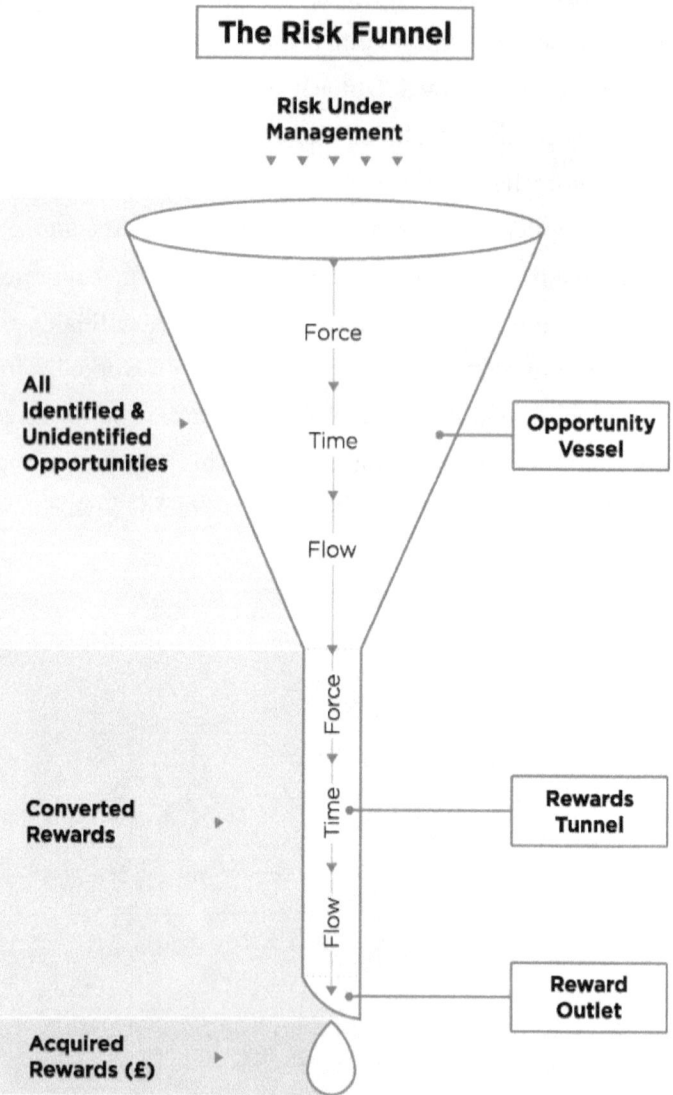

Figure 3: The Risk Funnel

A great example to demonstrate the workings of a risk funnel is an orange juice manufacturing plant. The process begins with crates of oranges being unloaded and sorted. (**Opportunity Vessel**) The oranges travel through various stages of washing, peeling, and juicing. The extracted juice is then filtered and poured into pre-labelled bottles. (**Between Opportunity Vessel and Reward Tunnel**). These bottles move seamlessly along the conveyor belt, passing through automated capping and sealing machines that ensure each bottle is securely closed. Further along, the bottles are meticulously inspected for quality control. Finally, the bottles of orange juice are neatly packed into cartons, and each carton is priced and stamped with a production date and batch number. (**Reward Tunnel**) The cartons are then placed on pallets, ready to be shipped out to stores and supermarkets at the wholesale price. From the processing plant to the consumer's table, this supply chain journey ensures that the orange juice reaches customers at the retail price. (**Reward Outlet**).

There are certain key features and factors worth noting:

- **Inclusivity of Opportunities:** All opportunities, whether clearly identified or vaguely recognised, are collected in the wide mouth of the funnel.

- **Commensurate Risk-Taking:** The process of applying Force, Time, and Flow indicates that necessary, adequate, and efficient risk-taking commensurate to each opportunity is vital. This includes risk management activities to protect the opportunity conversion process from threats and problem management.

- **Focused Effort:** The narrow spout represents the concentrated and deliberate effort of the risk-taker, whether a person or an entity, required to convert opportunities into rewards.

- **Opportunity Viscosity and Flow Rate:** Just as the viscosity of fluid affects how easily it flows through the funnel, the quality and nature of your opportunities can affect how easily and quickly they can be converted to rewards. The crucial factor for each opportunity is not necessarily speed but dynamism in your ability to use your resources with the factors required for processing opportunities (Force, Time, and Flow). The action you take affects the flow rate of what comes out of the opportunity. Flow rate is the outcome versus time. Now think about squeezing a toothpaste tube. The amount of paste that flows out and the time taken is dependent on your squeeze pressure.

- **Opportunity Resistance:** Opportunities will face resistance in the form of threats and problems. Ensure you perform scenario analysis as part of your risk management to identify all potential threats to your opportunities and put in place appropriate and adequate controls before you commence processing your opportunities. Some threats may materialise, and problems will arise. Prepare resolution plans and contingency plans. These should be developed as part of your scenario analysis before problems arise so that you can recover from them quickly and more meticulously whilst maintaining continuity to get to the end of the Risk Funnel stage.

CHAPTER TEN

Upgrading the World's Risk Operating System for a Better Future

The scene of this world has changed, and so must the operating systems we use to approach it. Evolving at an unprecedented pace, the need to be more conscious of risk-taking is crucial. Yet, the traditional approaches to risk, referred to as risk management, entrenched in the practices of risk management institutions, standards, and frameworks, are becoming increasingly obsolete. This has led the world into a rabbit hole from which it is unable and unwilling to reverse. Operating systems like the Committee of Sponsoring Organizations of the Treadway Commission's Enterprise Risk Management (COSO ERM) and the ISO 31000 Risk Management Guideline, among others, have primarily focused on risk as a negative phenomenon that often results in adverse outcomes. This misleading ideology results in countless unfulfilled purposes for both individuals and organisations. The methods relied on today are remnants of a bygone era, where the velocity of change was slower, and the stakes were not as high. As we stand on the brink of a future characterised by rapid technological advancements, global interconnectedness, and complex challenges, it is imperative that we upgrade the world's risk operating system.

The Current Mode of Operating Risk

Of the hundreds of people I asked to define risk in the course of writing this book, only about 10% were able to associate it with the possibility of both a good or bad outcome determined by a person's actions. Expand this globally, and you will get the same results. This largely reveals the disparity between the rich and the poor, the successful and the unsuccessful, the doers and the followers, the advanced and the less advanced, the purposeful ones and the aimless ones, and the list goes on.

Who is or are to blame for these disparities? You could say the individual, but then systems are wired a certain way, and most people are psychologically cajoled into a way of thinking that results in underperformance or undervalue. The way the world thinks and practices risk has been wrong for several centuries, with only the few who understand it better thriving at the expense of others and not revealing what they call secrets to success—until now that you have this book in your hands. The current mode of operating risk, known as risk management, has failed and continues to this day to fail to help people and businesses achieve their purpose.

When you think risk is bad all the time, the result you get is 'bad'. If you think risk is good or bad, then you have a chance at either. But when you think risk is tantamount to purpose, you can accomplish something greater. Risk today is primarily aimed at the process of controlling negative outcomes. It is understandable why it does not lead to the generation of rewards that support the achievement of purpose. Affiliated with outdated ways of thinking and struggling to keep up with the modern way of life and business, risk management alone cannot create the benefits needed to sustain the population of the world today. Neither does it provide an assured way for people and organisations to achieve their purpose until now, in this book.

For many organisations, these outdated risk management practices present bottlenecks, stifling innovation and agility. They are often rigid, bureaucratic, and excessively cautious, prioritising risk avoidance over opportunity exploration. In the face of today's dynamic landscape, this mindset is not only limiting but perilous. It has contributed to economic failures that make life difficult for people. The risk management institutions that exist today share responsibility for the poverty that exists in many lands, economic catastrophes, unequal wealth distribution, rising crime, health crises, geopolitical tension, and conflicts because they fail to show people how to take risks and achieve purpose.

Throughout this book, I have consistently shown you the why, what, who, where, and when of risk-taking that will help you achieve your purpose. As I bring this book to a close, I urge every reader to take a bold step in the right direction, starting by knowing the purpose you want to achieve that gives you a measure of freedom to live the life you want. The wisdom I have shared throughout this book is an upgraded operating system for risk that acknowledges the complexities of our world and promotes a holistic approach to risk-taking on the journey to achieving your purpose.

Risk —Risk Is a Person or an Entity with a Purpose

Risk is a person or an entity with a purpose. This means the risk is you! What you do as the risk determines the outcome you get in relation to your purpose. In the evolving landscape of today's world, continuing to think and act as though risk is just a mere hazard to be mitigated or an obstacle to be avoided will be a real mistake, leaving you not reaching your true potential. It is like being hungry and not knowing it until it is too late and you faint. Integrating the next level of risk that the world today needs to operate on—a system where risk is known as a person or any organisation with a defined purpose—is not just transformative but adaptive. This paradigm shift underscores the idea that risk is integral to the journey every individual and organisation needs to undergo to achieve its purpose.

Every human culture and entity, be they organisations, companies, or businesses, inherently recognises the need for accomplishment and takes a chance using the model they feel may work. This blind trust may occasionally yield some results but often is below par the potential possible. In the modern context, risk is about identifying potential opportunities and taking conscious actions to convert these opportunities into tangible rewards that are possible, as I have shown throughout this book. This proactive approach to risk can lead to significant progressive cultural and societal benefits for both human and organisational sustainability.

The integration and application of Risk 2.0 is beneficially far-reaching. For individuals, this is an awakening into a consciousness that can be best described as a symbolic 'coming out of the dark' that opens you up to opportunities that are all around you. Gaining this mastery, as laid out from the first chapter of this book, will be the only instrument you need to stay in the light. When you are hungry and see the fruit on the tree, you will find a way to climb that tree to get the fruit so you can eat and live. For organisations, this is the bringing together of 'collective purposes' to achieve a global purpose that serves the world better.

Risk 2.0 is scalable across various sectors and industries. In technology, it drives innovation and product development. In finance, it leads to wealth creation and economic sensibility. In healthcare, it pushes for advancements that improve patient care and outcomes. All sectors can reach their full potential and evolve into a greater purpose by integrating and applying Risk 2.0 as set out in this book.

This unveiled nature of risk ensures that the pursuit of purpose is not singular to oneself; its multiplicity lies in the connectedness to other purposes for future prosperity.

This century is by far the most disruptive in history. With advancements in many sectors, you might question: why is the world not integrated towards a better good for humanity? The world is one big company with many CEOs and their systems. For true potential to reveal itself, there needs to be an upgrade to a system that is functional and productive. Integration requires the restructuring of cultures and systems of operating the distribution of resources, the core of which are food, finance, health, technology, and governance. The state of fragility of the world mandates no time for trial-and-error tactics that may or may not yield rewards. We are risk-takers at birth; we have a purpose, and we need a roadmap to follow to achieve that purpose. Risk 2.0 gives the world a comprehensive risk operating system that can yield the rewards needed to empower each and every person and organisation to achieve the purpose they seek.

Conclusion

Many books have been written on risk, but none of them have timeless value. This book is different. What you have in your hand is a book that gives you hope that you can achieve your purpose. When you look at history, as far back as you can find surviving records, you see that wise and wealthy leaders took advantage of knowledge that the populace did not have or was not made known to them. They use ancient wisdom to create wealth and become visionaries.

The same is true today. Most people have not gained the wisdom that the top leaders of the world have used to create their wealth. Knowledge like this is strongly guarded so that they can remain at the top of their game, and they wow you with distilled speeches or courses that keep you where you are, never rising to their level of excellence. This curse is yours to break, and you have the way out with the open secret in this book. My aim is not to gain fame or fortune from this book but to share the truths about risk that I have found that can change lives for the better and transform organisations prosperously.

Julius Caesar's crossing of the Rubicon was a decisive act of defiance and ambition, encapsulating the essence of risk-taking that ultimately reshaped the Roman Republic into an empire. Caesar recognised that to leave a legacy they had to step beyond the boundaries of comfort zones and status quo and step into extreme self-stress testing situations and uncertainty to make a real difference in the world at that time signifying the wealth and power of the Roman Empire.

Today, some of the world's most influential leaders such as Donald J. Trump, Elon Musk, finance titans like JP Morgan's Jamie Dimon and many more are taking risks backed by wisdom they have acquired to shape the course of humanity in technology, finance, data, health and other aspects of life.

Your future starts the second you finish reading this line. You cannot 'unknow' the truths you have learned from this book. Take action now, upgrade your understanding of what risk really is, and acknowledge the risk-taker in you.

'The more you tell the truth, the stronger you become…
The more you lie, the weaker and more terrified you become.'
–Tucker Carlson

Acknowledgements

My God, Jehovah is your name. This book, with its wisdom, would not have been possible without your wisdom.

Lenora and Josh Owah for your continued motivation, encouragement - especially spiritually in 'the best life ever' that we share.

Ras Asur (fka Martin McKenzie), who helped me see things from a perspective I did not previously consider.

My Geography lecturer, Professor Joshua Ogbonna at Abia State University, who called us 'bubbleheads' when we did not perform to our full potential. Everything worked out for the best 30 years on.

My publisher, Cris Cawley and the Game Changer Publishing team, thank you for that 'out of the blue' first Twitter (X) message urging me to write a book. I'm glad to be working with you.

To the people who stress-tested me in good and bad ways, thank you for the data (experiences) that helped me develop the thinking ability to transform and continue to 'evolve my brain'.

And finally, my intellectual sparring partner Sebastian Jung on this journey of transforming the world of risk.

Also by Chizubel E. Beluchi

For the love of Purpose

The Risk Champs Podcast

THANK YOU FOR READING MY BOOK!

The Secret Chapter
(Bonus Gift!)

Just to say thanks for buying and reading my book, I would like to give you a bonus gift, no strings attached!

I wrote this extra chapter as a bonus gift to you to fast-track the value you get from reading this book.

Scan the QR code:

I appreciate your interest in my book, and value your feedback as it helps me improve future versions of this book. I would appreciate it if you could leave your invaluable review on Amazon.com with your feedback. Thank you!

www.ingramcontent.com/pod-product-compliance
Lightning Source LLC
Chambersburg PA
CBHW021113130626
46554CB00002B/662